THE
SOCIAL
SINGULARITY

SOCIAL
EVOLUTION

THE
SOCIAL
SINGULARITY

A Decentralist Manifesto

MAX BORDERS

For more information, visit
http://social-evolution.com

To
Justin
and Jessica
Arman
because they believe

CONTENTS

INTRODUCTION

For an undetermined period of
time I felt myself cut off from the
world, an abstract spectator....
The road kept descending and
branching off, through meadows
misty in the twilight.
          —Jorge Luis Borges[1]

WE HAVE ALWAYS TRIED to know tomorrow. In our attempts, we end up
shaping it.

Our ancestors went to seers who read tea leaves, auras, or entrails. To best an
enemy or win a lover, rulers consulted oracles for messages from the gods. Oracles in antiquity were thought to be divinely inspired, so false predictions were
blamed on bad interpretation.

Modern oracles are decidedly more fallible. We're also more accountable. So
we look for patterns in the world beyond the guts, and we channel the god of
trend lines. Still, we make predictions we hope will come true, which is often
why we make them to start with.

Today they call us futurists. But to be a futurist still takes a little mysticism. It's
not the vagueness of Nostradamus or the Magick of Aleister Crowley but the
spark of the science-fiction writer who plants ideas in the minds of innovators.

Futurists know that in every prediction there is a potential act of creation. After
all people who believe our predictions are more likely to change. And if enough
people change, the world might just get better. In *The Social Singularity*, I'll
show that the world's power centers are breaking up and that this process can

liberate people from poverty, end acrimonious politics, and help humanity avoid the robot apocalypse. I realize that's a tall order. But that's just how much potential there is in decentralization.

Decentralization?

This is the kind of big, abstract idea editors warn could mean the death of your book sales. *Write about a person or tell a story*, they'll say, chomping on the end of a spent cigar. *I can't sell a book about an abstraction!* Well, we've got to try. The future depends on it.

In this volume, I suggest that if we reorganize ourselves and our systems of collective intelligence, we will be better as a species. The social singularity is a point beyond which humanity will have reoriented itself. We'll operate more like a hive mind.

A lot of people are afraid of what's to come. But to live in fear of the future is to underestimate ourselves. So this book is also about shedding fear.

Still, it's not your basic airplane read. It's designed to challenge you. To break conventions. To reframe our thinking a little so as to disrupt the habits of mind that are keeping all of us from reaching our full potential. You see, our march toward the social singularity will be largely positive.

Yes, there will be a great economic churn thanks to artificial intelligence and automation. Of course, there is always the risk of future shock,[2] and people will still carry within them the urge to control, to centralize, and to "rage for order."[3] But technology is helping us to become far more collaborative, and there is more ordering power in that force than in any demagogue with a standing army.

I'm not a passive chronicler of events. Behind this book lies a deeper purpose —a mission that is the wellspring of my thinking. If you're comfortable with all these caveats, I invite you to join me in exploring a new set of forking paths into the future. For as soon as we take those first steps on any path, we're engaging in acts of creation, for better or for worse.

CHAPTER ONE

THE END OF POLITICS

The spectacle is not a collection
of images, but a social relation
among people, mediated by
images.
— Guy Debord[4]

IF YOU'RE READING THIS, chances are you own some sort of mobile computing device. Maybe you haven't given up paper books entirely, but you're surely tethered. I suspect you check your device at least twice a day, if not twice an hour. And I'd bet you have at least fifty apps.

Now imagine you wake up one morning, turn on your device, and realize everything has changed. Where before there were fifty or more applications, there are now only two: a red app and a blue app. It seems the apps compete for processing power so now the device runs more slowly and less efficiently. And on this operating system—call it "DOS," or Democratic Operating System—only the red app and the blue app run. Though the device advertises compatibility with other apps, everybody finds DOS only seems to work with the red one and the blue one.

You are understandably frustrated with your device, especially as you remember a time when it ran much better, had far more options, and allowed you to customize it according to your needs and preferences.

This thought experiment is meant to help us reflect on our sociopolitical status quo. Not on who's in charge, not on the next election, but rather upon the system itself. Why? Because there seems to be a collective illusion that a democratic republic is as good as it gets. After all, we haven't yet really tried anything beyond DOS. And there seems to be a near-universal failure of imagina-tion with respect to how we could do better.

In a 1947 speech, Winston Churchill made his now-famous assessment:

> Many forms of Government have been tried and will be tried in this world of sin and woe. No one pretends that democracy is perfect or all-wise. Indeed, it has been said that democracy is the worst form of government except all those other forms that have been tried from time to time.[5]

This is the sort of fatalism most people accept. In fact, almost no one tries to imagine another social operating system. The most creative and ambitious ideas for social change almost always happen *within* DOS: We should pass law X or adopt policy Y. Very few are trying to figure out how to develop something en-tirely new that circumvents politics entirely or, at least, fundamentally changes it.

It should be clear by now that I'm not interested in preserving the status quo. We can do better—and we must, because DOS's days are numbered.

For a lot of people, this will be unsettling.

Some readers will scoff. Others will worry I'm trying to rock a boat that's keep-ing billions of people afloat. Still others will say I'm an anarchist, a utopian, or a dreamer. And we should no doubt treat with great respect the system that took us from bullets to ballots. The democratic republic has become the most pros-perous and arguably peaceful way to organize society the world has seen. So it's no wonder smart people like Francis Fukuyama have argued that the demo-cratic republic was the form on which most of the countries of the world would eventually settle. There is a lot to recommend about this form, particularly when considered in the arc of history.

But there is a lot wrong with DOS. And whatever happens after DOS should be a welcome upgrade that addresses what doesn't work about this particular so-cial operating system, all while introducing new functions, new features, and a new paradigm of human social interaction.

The Best of Enemies

The most salient problem with our current form of governance is its symptoms. One of those symptoms is that politics tends to make us, ahem, ungracious.

Recall the famous 1968 televised debates between William F. Buckley, Jr., and Gore Vidal, a conservative and a liberal. The whole thing culminates in a moment where—after a heated exchange—Buckley, taking Vidal's bait, explodes:

"Now listen, you queer, stop calling me a crypto-Nazi, or I'll sock you in the goddamn face and you'll stay plastered."

And there it was. The dandies of the Left and Right reduced to ad hominem attacks, almost coming to blows. Nielsen loved it because ratings soared. And politics as prime-time blood sport became an American pastime.

Matters only got worse with the arrival of the Internet. What we thought would be a tool to bring out the best in us, such as creativity and collaboration (which it has been), has also become a platform from which people can hurl insults at those with whom they disagree, then easily retreat into partisan echo chambers.

According to a documentary about Buckley and Vidal called *The Best of Enemies*, both died with the poison of political and personal animus still in their spleens. And as Americans continue with politics basically unchanged—though with social media magnifying any spectacle and offering everyone a bullhorn—the symptoms of partisanship are getting worse every year.

This polarization is happening to all of us.

As the political parade passes, people gather to watch the show, choosing their sides of the boulevard. In so choosing, they self-segregate. Tribal affiliations are on display. It's a natural human tendency with deep roots in our evolutionary past.

In an experiment,[6] even people predisposed to favor members of their own race turned out to be biased in favor of people randomly assigned to wear the same team's basketball jersey as they were—even when those people were of different races—and against even people of the same race if they were wearing a different team's colors. As science journalist Sharon Begley points out, we team up with people according to "whether they are likely to be an ally or an enemy." That illustrates how tribal we are. We are wired to be divided.

Politics brings out the worst in us by tapping into these tribal tendencies. Sure, trading barbs is better than trading bullets. We all know really nice people who participate in stinging or acrimonious exchanges online. Maybe we do it ourselves.

Here's a headline you might have shared: "5 Scientific Studies That Prove Republicans Are Stupid." Or: "Yes, Liberalism is a Mental Disorder." In the United States, that's more than 300 million people who are either stupid or crazy. Few want to acknowledge that it might be stupid or crazy to make such claims or for a country to divide itself this way. But in America, at least, it's effectively a two-party system. So in DOS you have two choices of app, which means two basic choices of tribal affiliation.

The Worst in Us

I used to wonder whether anybody besides H. L. Mencken saw things this way. I found the following from legal analyst Trevor Burrus:

> Like any other game, the rules create the attitudes and strategies of the players. Throw two brothers into the Colosseum for a gladiatorial fight to the death, and brotherly sentiment will quickly evaporate. Throw siblings, neighbors, or friends into a political world that increasingly controls our deepest values, and love and care are quickly traded for resentment.[7]

It's true. From a very young age, we're told that when breaking bread with friends and family, politics and religion are verboten. But it's not just that it will put relationships at risk, says Burrus. Democratic politics turns a continuum of possibilities into stark, binary choices. Tribal teams coalesce around linear, black-and-white thinking as our biases take over.

> Now that we've invented a problem—"which group of 50 percent +1 will control education for everyone?"—imposed a binary solution—"we will teach either creation or evolution"—and invented teams to rally around those solutions —"are you a science denier or a science supporter?"—our

tribal and self-serving brains go to work assuring us that we
are on the side of righteousness and truth.[8]

All these woeful debates become increasingly shrill. When it all reaches fever
pitch, virtue signalers pen pleas for greater tolerance and more reasoned discourse. But it does no good. Tribal brains burn hotter than any of these appeals
for civility. Until we change the rules, we're not likely to find changes in ourselves.

Again, I admit that when compared to tyranny and war, partisan politics ain't so
bad. But what if something else came along? Wouldn't we start to see democracy as a golden calf?

Politics—especially during federal elections—creates a system that brings out
the worst in people. It poisons relationships. It pulls us in as spectators who
stand agog at a completely inauthentic show of national politics over which any
one of us has virtually no power. We end up mostly ignoring local issues over
which we could have considerably more influence. As a consequence, an entire
nation falls under a particular kind of spell.

The only people to whom our opinions really matter are the pollsters, with their
wet fingers held aloft, and the media, who hold up mirrors so distorted we can
barely recognize ourselves.

People are different. They are going to have differences of opinion, hold different values, and run in different circles. This is a fact. But we expect that a
monolith of partisan opinion should extend to a nation of 350 million people—
by brute force if necessary. And until they do, we'll just get on social media and
sock them in the face until they stay plastered.

On Election Day, the team with the red jerseys will pull on its side of the rope.
The team with the blue jerseys will pull on its side of the rope. In the end, both
will end up the mud—because they've been standing in it all along.

Hobbits and Hooligans

What may be as disconcerting as the kind of people politics turns us into are the
types of voters in whose hands we have placed democracy. Political philosopher Jason Brennan names these creatures "hobbits" and "hooligans." He
writes:

> Hobbits are mostly apathetic and ignorant about politics.
> They lack strong, fixed opinions about most political is-
> sues. Often they have no opinions at all. They have little, if
> any, social scientific knowledge; they are ignorant not just
> of current events but also of the social scientific theories
> and data needed to evaluate as well as understand these
> events.[9]

In this way, hobbits are almost as indifferent to politics as they are ignorant of the issues. Brennan reminds us that the typical nonvoter is a hobbit, which makes it odd that anyone would want to encourage nonvoters to vote for any reason beyond the most cynical. On the other hand, when we consider that many people who end up voting are probably also hobbits, we have to wonder about the arbitrariness of it all. After all, why should people who have no knowledge of or interest in social-scientific data or world history have any say in the rules you live by?

The rest of those who decide the fate of nations Brennan calls "hooligans."

> Hooligans are the rabid sports fans of politics. They have
> strong and largely fixed worldviews. They can present ar-
> guments for their beliefs, but they cannot explain alterna-
> tive points of view in a way that people with other views
> would find satisfactory. Hooligans consume political infor-
> mation, although in a biased way.[10]

You probably recognize hooligans from social media. They seek articles that confirm their preexisting opinions, but, writes Brennan, they "ignore, evade, and reject out of hand evidence that contradicts or disconfirms their preexisting opinions."[11] Thus data is only good to hooligans insofar as it supports their views.

It's not just that hooligans zealously form political opinions based on their tribal affiliations and confirmation biases; it's also that their tribal membership forms their very identity, which in the United States shores up DOS and its two apps. In such a polarized climate, hooligans "tend to despise people who dis-agree with them, holding that people with alternative worldviews are stupid, evil, selfish, or at best, deeply misguided."

When we consider that the great bulk of the voting population is made up of people who either know very little about anything (and don't really care) or only want to know things that confirm what they already believe, we've got a system that runs primarily on a mix of ignorance and ideology. Between elections, hooligans are beating each other up at rallies or shutting down speeches on campuses. Hobbits are going about their lives, from time to time wondering what all the fuss is about.

When we think about having our collective fate determined this way, it should also strike us that democracy is quite arbitrary. But it's also arbitrary beyond those who participate. To understand that arbitrariness, we have first to unpack it. The late comedian George Carlin provided two relevant nuggets of wisdom. He said he doesn't vote because "it's meaningless," and he said the United States was "bought and paid" for a long time ago. Let's take each of Carlin's nuggets of wisdom in turn.

A Teardrop in the Ocean

First, we have to face the grim truth that our vote doesn't count. I realize that in fourth grade Mrs. Crabtree taught us that voting lets our *voices be heard*. But that's not really true. It is akin to thinking the drummer hears you when you yell at him from the nosebleed seats of Madison Square Garden. The purveyors of these sorts of untruths probably don't realize they're spreading untruths. If they do, they think they're only repeating little white lies—like telling a child Santa Claus is real.

But Santa Claus isn't real. Your vote doesn't count. Crying a single teardrop into the ocean will not determine the fate of high tide, and the drummer playing Madison Square Garden can't hear you scream.

To be fair, though, some brilliant people disagree. Techno-evangelist Clay Shirky thinks democracy is the best we've got right now, so we're duty bound to rock the vote. Not a protest vote, either. You *have* to pick the red app or the blue app.

"It doesn't matter what message you think you are sending, because no one will receive it. No one is listening," writes Shirky. "The system is set up so that every choice other than 'R' or 'D' boils down to 'I defer to the judgement of my fellow citizens.' It's easy to argue that our system shouldn't work like that. It's impossible to argue it doesn't work like that."[12]

The problem with Shirky's claim is it doesn't matter how you vote. Even if you vote "R" or "D," no one is listening. One might argue matters are slightly improved in a parliamentary system. But not in the US.

According to NBC News, only people in Colorado, Iowa, Nevada, New Hampshire, North Carolina, Ohio, Pennsylvania, and Virginia had anything but an infinitesimal chance that their vote would affect the outcome of the 2016 presidential election.[13]

Any given voter had a better chance of being struck by lightning on the way to the voting booth. As *Forbes* columnist Jim Pagels puts it: "The most generous estimates claim you have a 1-in-10-million chance of being the deciding vote in [a presidential] election, and that's only if you live in a swing state and if you vote for one of the two major parties. Overall, the estimate is roughly 1-in-60 million."[14]

Let that sink in for a moment.

You're almost 100 percent assured you could switch your vote in every major election throughout your life and the outcome would be the same. Following Carlin, then, your vote is "meaningless." Or as political philosopher Jason Brennan notes, "telling someone they can't complain about an election if they didn't vote is akin to telling a homeless person that they can't complain about being poor unless they play the lottery every day."[15]

Ouch. But matters are even worse.

The Unicorn Problem

Duke University political economist Michael Munger deepens our political nihilism with what he calls the "Unicorn Problem." The problem is not just with voting, he explains. It's with the very idea of the state as a steward of the true, the beautiful and the good. Munger continues: "If you want to advocate the use of unicorns as motors for public transit, it is important that unicorns actually exist, rather than only existing in your imagination. People immediately understand why relying on imaginary creatures would be a problem in practical mass transit."

But most people can't see why the government they imagine is a unicorn. So to help them, Munger proposes what he humbly calls "the Munger test":

1. Go ahead, make your argument for what you want the State to do, and what you want the State to be in charge of [or the "message" you want to send].

2. Then, go back and look at your statement. Everywhere you said "the State," delete that phrase and replace it with "politicians I actually know, running in electoral systems with voters and interest groups that actually exist."

3. If you still believe your statement, then we have something to talk about.[16]

Munger admits to entertaining himself with this rhetorical device: "When someone says, 'The State should be in charge of hundreds of thousands of heavily armed troops, with the authority to use that coercive power,' ask them to take out the unicorn ('the State') and replace it with [the politician you most dislike]. How do you like it now?"[17]

When democracy advocates say the only way to "send a message" is to vote for one of the two parties, they have fallen victim to the unicorn fallacy. It's not just that your message likely won't be received if you do vote; it's that it will be crumpled up and thrown into a dumpster on K Street[18] by people you *know* you would never want making the rules on your behalf.

Why People Vote

Apart from the illusion that "your vote matters" or "your voice is heard," why do people vote?

Most folks don't really think their votes will have an appreciable effect. So why do they vote? Here are three big reasons:

- **Declarative-Expressive:** People vote to express themselves, whatever it is they're expressing, because the immediate cost of doing so is negligible;
- **Ideological-Utopian:** People vote in accordance with some abstraction—a wished-for state-of-affairs, ideal, or unrealizable utopia;
- **Tribal-Coalitional:** People vote in solidarity with those they perceive as their ingroup, team, or tribe.

As you might have figured out, these are some of the psychological bases of political hooliganism.

But you might be wondering: What about people who are interested only in the truth? What about people who are calm, rational, and willing to suspend judgment about candidates and policies until they have enough information to determine logically whether said candidates and policies will work in the interests of the public good?

Brennan calls these types "vulcans." And they are as rare as they are irrelevant. Maybe we can imagine a system in which only vulcans could vote, say, after passing some vulcan exam acceptable as a standard by nonvulcans. But even if you could get beyond the inherent elitism in such a suggestion, it's not clear that any social science wielded by vulcans would generate a better form of government.

Science writer Ron Bailey reminds us that most experts can't be trusted, and that statisticians like John Ioannidis have been sounding the alarm as far back as 2005. Ioannidis found that "in most fields of research, including biomedicine, genetics, and epidemiology, the research community has been terrible at weeding out the shoddy work largely due to perfunctory peer review and a paucity of attempts at experimental replication."[19] Ioannidis's conclusion? "Most published research findings are false."

Biomedicine? Genetics? Epidemiology? These areas are supposed to be relatively close to the hard sciences. These aren't squishier social sciences like economics, social psychology, and political science.

In response to democracy's shortcomings, Brennan proposes a system he terms "epistocracy," which suggests governance by those who are slightly more competent on matters with which they are more familiar. We should be leery of Brennan's proposal, though not because life wouldn't be marginally better than it is under the system we have now. Maybe things would be better for a time. We should be leery of epistocracy just as we should be leery of any platoon of philosopher-kings wielding stats. After all, there are lots of hooligans masquerading as vulcans, particularly in the academy.

Epistocracy risks morphing into just another contrivance of centralized thinking, even if it seems marginally to decentralize voting. There are many more interesting alternatives on the horizon. But let's not get ahead of ourselves. Giving people voting power over domains of activity in which they claim to be experts risks technocracy, as it opens the door to a tyranny of experts. Though

Brennan's critique of democracy is dead on, his suggested upgrade leaves something to be desired.

Now let's turn to George Carlin's second nugget of wisdom: the idea that US politics was bought and sold a long time ago.

Politics without Romance

Why do politicians constantly disappoint us? Late Nobel laureate James Buchanan more or less set out to answer this question in his life's work. Buchanan was one of the founders of the public-choice school of political economy. And in a single essay called "Politics without Romance," Buchanan lays out his general thesis in cold, dispassionate terms:

> If the government is empowered to grant monopoly rights or tariff protection to one group, at the expense of the general public or of designated losers, it follows that potential beneficiaries will compete for the prize. And since only one group can be rewarded, the resources invested by other groups—which could have been used to produce valued goods and services—are wasted.[20]

Those who are supposed to represent you are playing a game that tends to benefit favored groups (read: not you).

> Much of the growth of the bureaucratic or regulatory sector of government can best be explained in terms of the competition between political agents for constituency support through the use of promises of discriminatory transfers of wealth.[21]

As much as we wish the forces Buchanan identifies weren't the most powerful forces in politics, to think otherwise would be, well, romantic.

If the Munger test reminds us that people you don't like hold actual power, public-choice economics reminds us that people we don't like get power and then auction it off to corporate or bureaucratic interests. In other words, once all the hobbits' and hooligans' teardrops have been counted, the incentives of the democratic republic are less about those creatures' good and more about money and power mixing to gain advantages in their respective domains.

That's why money and power are so attracted to each other. Even the most ardent do-gooder in office has to engage in horse-trading to get anything done. You might call it selling out. She might call it political survival.

Local Knowledge

From time to time, politicians do try to do what they think is in the public interest. That is difficult, though. What after all is "the public" but a whole lot of people, each of whom differs from the others? And why should a lawyer from Manhattan have anything to say about the operations of a ranch outside Missoula?

As our society becomes more complex, it becomes even less plausible to think that people in distant capitals have the requisite knowledge to plan for anything so far away from their spheres of understanding. And this is true even if the people in question are Brennan's vulcans. As Friedrich A. Hayek famously reminds us, science is not the sum of knowledge. Most of the important stuff we know involves particular circumstances and contexts.

Knowledge of specific circumstances, or "local knowledge," is the most important and overlooked feature of complex societies. And as we become more complex, we will have to develop sense-making apparatuses and forms of collective intelligence that can handle this complexity. People in government, well-intentioned as they might be, are woefully ill equipped to make judgments about people in local circumstances.

Even if we don't need central control and planning in our increasingly complex society, we still need governance. Someday, though, we'll look back on politics and shake our heads. It will have been a necessary phase—but not one we'll want to relive. We have been undergoing a series of phases we could not have bypassed.

The good news is we may have already entered the next phase. Once we realize all the benefits of this next phase, we'll see how wasteful and acrimonious politics has been.

Trench Warfare

Right now it doesn't seem like we are headed for a post-political era. Most people are so locked into the political paradigm that arguments about who is to fund whose birth control—or whether the city school system should get another bond—seem bigger than life. Each side cedes mere inches back and forth between election cycles in a kind of trench warfare. Such is the nature of politics. And in politics, the only thing we share anymore is a desire to take and hold onto power.

The party that has the ring rules the land, at least for a while. The other side snatches power back sooner or later, and the whole thing starts all over again. Yet each side's adherents labor under the idea that if they can just get and keep the ring, they will use it to good ends. *We'll give it to the right people,* they imagine. *The right people are incorruptible.*

We're still waiting for the right people.

So we go back to that titanic tug of war. Time and energy we could use on creative activities we spend locked in counterproductive struggles. We polarize. We argue. Our tribal-coalitional natures—as well as our unwavering belief in our own laundry lists of values and virtues—divide us in ways that go deeper than party affiliation. One side wants to take away the guns and the sugary sodas, the other wants to pray away the gay. The rest of us simply hang out at the margins. People can scarcely talk to each other without spitting venom. If there are any beneficiaries to this tit-for-tat, they're rarely the ones who send their prayers up in the voting booth. A parasite class of special interests reaps most of the rewards, because the real action is on K Street. For the rest of us, politics is at best a spectacle, a kind of team sport.

Was all this struggle necessary?

Yes. And again, there has been virtue in such a zero-sum game. Politics is a way to fight somewhat humanely over the control of hierarchy. The American Republic was in certain respects designed to create checks between factions and parties by setting them against each other. Ballots beat bullets and all that. It was thought of as a necessary evil—an alternative to the subjugation of people, which came from monarchy, feudalism, and aristocratic privilege.

In the *Federalist Papers,* James Madison expressed concern about the "mischiefs of faction" found in democracies of various sizes. The Constitution is designed to temper the consequences of faction, even as the man known as its father acknowledged that the "causes of faction cannot be removed."[22] The democratic republic was thus a kind of rationally conceived operating system, forged in compromise after a revolution provided an opportunity to start fresh.

From another perspective, the development of the American-style republic was a *phase transition*. In other words, the democratic republic was likely to have arisen at some point due to the world's becoming more complex. Some revere the founding as the explication of timeless principles the founders discovered using reason. And yet we know the founders were crafting rules at a certain stage of technological development and in a certain historical context. They were moving headlong into a future informed by reasonable assumptions about human nature and the new circumstances in which people found themselves. To understand this stage and prior stages, it will benefit us first to take our time machine a little further into the past, then zip back.

The Rise of Hierarchy

For millennia, our ancestors roamed the African steppe. Early humans were hunter-gatherers, anthropologists say. And as those ancestors succeeded at hunting and gathering, their numbers grew. But the world was no Garden of Eden for long, if it ever was. Life became nasty, brutish, and short. As their numbers grew, these tribal bands eventually confronted life-threatening scarcities. And Thomas Malthus's warning, an error when he introduced it in 1789, was more or less correct back in the Paleolithic period: Success in procreating meant the land would reach its carrying capacity. To avoid Malthus's trap, early folk had to move about. Their migrations contributed to the world's great peopling.

As early humans moved around, they collided. There was fierce competition for available resources. Peoples faced off in bloody conflict. Intertribal warfare meant the hunter-gatherer tribes had to become warrior clans. They not only had to learn to fight and kill, but they also had to learn to *organize themselves* to fight together better. None of this is meant to suggest that early peoples did not trade peacefully across tribes. Many did. But those who did not become traders were raiders.

Such a harsh state of affairs meant that, to survive, your tribe had to develop better social technology. That doesn't mean Windows for Cavemen. Social technology is shorthand for *how people organize themselves*. Victors transmitted their stories of glory and successful warfare strategies into the future. Likewise, while strength, courage, and superior weaponry go a very long way, social technology could make or break clan society.

Agriculture and statecraft helped to settle some of these fighter-nomads. With settling came civilization. Still, much of history since the world's great peopling has nevertheless been a story of warfare. After all, civilization often comes with wealth and power.

In the simultaneous development of warfare and civilization, one social technology came to dominate: hierarchy. Atop this form of organization there usually stood one person. This leader went by many names—chief, king, warlord—but to succeed, the chief would have to be capable of gaining the fear, respect, and loyalty of his people. In accepting this leader, the clan would have gained an advantage. Having enabled a skilled strategist to command them as a force, they could operate as a single, fierce unit. That would be a recipe for survival and glory in an age of conquest.

Of course, those capable of such fierceness and cunning were also capable of suppressing dissent. Those who wished to survive in the order were likely to accept the order, that being preferable to slaughter.

Great empires soon grew up amid the detritus of war. The clan king became a god-king. The administration of empire required more layers of hierarchy, which meant delegating power to satraps and governors. The emperor would issue commands to subordinates, and those commands would be carried out by *their* subordinates in the chain of command. Patronage relationships became the norm. The order of those lording power over others took on religious dimensions. Values such as loyalty, honor, obedience, and patriotism firmed up the hierarchy. Without such values, the structure could have been weakened by either internal dissent or better-organized enemies.

Hierarchy became more elaborate over time as each layer was added, and hierarchy persisted, apparently, as humanity's dominant social technology.

Despite a couple of eighteenth-century revolutions in France and America, hierarchy is still, in many respects, the dominant form of social organization throughout the world. That is, social structures like those of medieval Europe and feudal Japan are more common than those like modern Switzerland's. Even modern Japan and Switzerland still have command-and-control structures. The United States—that great beacon of freedom—now bears a striking resemblance to the Roman Empire. America's founders had made improvements by creating institutional checks and balances on power within its hierarchy. But its hierarchy persists. The question then: Is it long for this world?

Better All the Time

Now to the present. There is no doubt too much war in the world today. The good news, however, is that the human race is entering an unprecedented age of peace, connection, and prosperity. I realize you probably didn't get that news on social media.

The "Great Fact," however, is that since about 1800, we've been growing more and more prosperous.[23] It's all thanks to an ongoing process of decentralization in which humanity reaps the rewards of innovation, production, and trade. More and more of the world runs on adaptive, lateral relationships instead of command-and-control structures and on open systems instead of closed ones. Nested networks of flourishing communities abound, and they are challenging the hierarchies around them. Such hierarchies include corporations, those old structures that pay you to be part of a hierarchy; they are starting to change. What should puzzle us is whether these nested networks exist *despite* or *because of* prevailing national hierarchies. Paradoxically, the answer could be "both," depending on where and when in the world we look.

To read the news, though, you wouldn't think anybody could claim things are getting better. The media sell more turmoil than they offer positive trends over longer timescales. Their reports leave many of us with both a false impression and a general ignorance about just how good we've got it compared to people throughout most of history.

Writer and cognitive scientist Steven Pinker is one of the most famous voices pointing out that the trendlines are mostly positive. In an interview with *New Scientist*, Pinker admits being struck by a graph that showed a precipitous decline in homicide rates in British towns, starting in the fourteenth century.

"The rates had plummeted by between 30 and 100-fold," said Pinker. "That stuck with me, because you tend to have an image of medieval times with happy peasants coexisting in close-knit communities, whereas we think of the present as filled with school shootings and mugging and terrorist attacks."[24]

In the era of sensational headlines traveling virally through social media horrible things can seem more frequent, bigger than life. So Pinker decided to do some more digging, and he learned that even twentieth-century Germany had a low rate of war deaths by comparison to the hunter-gatherers.[25]

From the perspective of history's grand sweep, we're living in an age of peace, freedom and abundance.

Even the poorest places on earth are far better off than they were just a few decades ago. Indeed, in the last thirty years alone, the number of people living in abject poverty has been cut in half. Day by day, violent aggression over resources is rapidly being replaced by the structures of commercial competition and human cooperation.

Commercial competition creates a positive-sum world—that is, a world of ever-increasing wealth. Today, the struggles are often among companies competing to offer, say, better gadgets. Small businesses are battling it out at the intersection of Third and Main to serve a better taco, brew a craftier beer, or open a hotter nightclub. The benefits flow to the customers and those who serve them best. All exist in an ecosystem of value.

In this more benevolent form of competition a fundamental truth remains: The fittest social technology will survive. Over time—as conquest culture has given way to commercial culture—we have come to see fewer warlords, kings, and emperors, and more bosses, executives, and CEOs. To some, this may not sound like such a big improvement. The competition is still fierce. Companies are still frequently cast as villainous exploiters, sometimes for good reason. But shifting from conquest to commerce has resulted in more people enjoying more good things than at any time in human history. And it's only getting better.

But in this transition, we have to ask: Will CEOs and middle managers also go the way of kings and lords?

The modern nation-state and the modern corporation share social technologies that go back thousands of years. But in between hierarchical governments and hierarchical firms, there is a great teeming. It is not chaos. People truck, barter, exchange, collaborate, and cooperate. In some cases—such as Morning Star Packing Company and Zappos—a phase transition has already been made.

Outside the firm, community groups meet over potluck dinners planned online. Friends find each other in dive bars and country clubs. Husbands and wives go home to one another; the bills get paid, and the kids get to school. Lovers find each other online in a kind of dating anarchy. And all of it happens without a director or a designer, a beautiful, unconducted symphony like starlings in a murmuration. More and more of the world operates in a place between rigid order and errant chaos—unmanaged yet orderly.

More and more of the world is self-organizing.

Phase Transition

Complexity science predicts the global trend to which I alluded above. At the risk of oversimplifying, the theory states "complexity transitions" will happen according to the amount and type of information flowing through a system. (A "system," in this sense, is a collection of devices or people that information gets transmitted among.) How elements of a system *deal* with information and resources—or, in the case of firms, knowledge and decisions—will determine the nature of that system.

Because systems always exist in some environment, often competing with other systems, evolutionary pressures are going to determine whether an organization such as your club, company, county, or country survives. And one of the traits selected for will be how well it coordinates its participants' behavior—which largely means: how well it organizes information.

Complexity science shows that to deal with more information, systems have to change. The process starts with a group growing big enough to form a hierarchy. This usually happens when the group has outgrown the organizational limits of the egalitarian clan structure. As more power gets delegated, extending the chains of hierarchy, the system becomes more complicated. But the hierarchy can only handle so much complication. Eventually the system breaks down or changes into something that looks more like a network with an increasing number of "nodes." Lateral relationships form, which we know as "peer to peer." Decision-making power spreads down and out. And this hastens the complexity transition.

Yaneer Bar-Yam (literally) wrote the textbook on complex systems. He describes the process that unfolded historically: "Ancient empires replaced various smaller kingdoms that had developed during a process of consolidation of yet smaller associations of human beings. The degree of control in these systems varied, but the progression toward larger more centrally controlled entities is apparent. . . . This led to a decrease of complexity of behaviors of many individuals, but a more complex behavior on the larger scale."[26]

But this could only be sustained for so long. As time went on, any given indi- vidual's behavior diversified, and so did all the tasks performed by everyone in the system. Such is the overall behavior of a system becoming more compli- cated. More complicated systems required "adding layers of management that served to exercise local control," explains Bar-Yam. "As viewed by the higher levels of management, each layer simplified the behavior to the point where an individual could control it. The hierarchy acts as a mechanism for communica- tion of information to and from management."[27]

But how far can introducing layers of management be sustained? When you reach the "point at which the collective complexity is the maximum individual complexity, the process breaks down,"[28] Bar-Yam adds. Hierarchical structures cannot handle any more complexity beyond this point.

Complexity science tells us the battle lines will be drawn mainly in terms of how each organization processes information and applies knowledge to make decisions. And if there is a way for an organization to deal with complexity be- yond hierarchy, that form of organization is poised to challenge the reigning paradigm.

So, if we put our ears to the ground, we can hear the rumbling of two great or- ganizational types: one that looks more like a hierarchy and one that looks more like a network.

Hierarchy still dominates. It is powerful—especially as it appeals to the human desire to be in control. And, of course, human beings have evolved dispositions to be led—whether by dictators, daddies, demagogues, or divas. Consciously or unconsciously, people in hierarchical organizations will also fight for the status quo as long as they benefit from it. It's human nature.

Yet, decentralized systems can be more flexible, and as thinker and writer Nas- sim Taleb observes, "antifragile." So the question remains: Which form will win? Before trying to answer that question, I want to leave you with more than just the image of clashing social technologies. Because what we're really inter- ested in here is flourishing or, more specifically, how people can organize themselves to improve their well-being. The extent to which we can organize ourselves to be happier, healthier people is the extent to which we can organize ourselves to create more peace and prosperity. Hard to believe? Despite some of the wrenching changes that will be brought about by this coming clash of systems, a more abundant and humane world awaits.

Founding Redux

In thinking about phase transition, though, the American founding still looms large. The American Republic and many democratic republics since were brilliantly crafted systems designed to maximize freedom and limit the excesses of hierarchy. Or, put another way, documents like the US Constitution put forth answers to the question, What sort of political order can be created to unleash as much human autonomy as possible?

But our operating system, as operating systems will, has become buggy, strained, and outdated. Not only are people becoming weary of a system designed to pit people against each other with a crude majoritarian calculus, but new systems are being developed to accommodate phase transition. Indeed, some of these systems don't require the permission of authorities. They arise from technologically connected people along the lines of what James C. Scott describes in *Two Cheers for Anarchism*.

> More regimes have been brought, piecemeal, to their knees by what was once called "Irish Democracy," the silent, dogged resistance, withdrawal, and truculence of millions of ordinary people, than by revolutionary vanguards or rioting mobs.[29]

Some will try to argue that an uncorrupted social operating system, i.e. the one originally conceived by the founders, would be a lot better than the version we have now—adulterated as it has been by dubious legal interpretation. I'm sympathetic to that view. But it would be difficult, if not impossible, to debug the program and bring back the founders' Constitution. And happily, we have better options.

For the first time in history, technology and culture are providing more and more opportunities to create new systems and migrate among them. Indeed, it used to be that to change systems, one had to migrate quite literally, to pick oneself up and move to another jurisdiction. And that, too, is an increasingly viable option. But migrating between systems is also something that, these days, you can do from your sofa. And this ease has profound implications.

The Authoritarian Urge

Before closing this chapter, we should give a final doff of the hat to the democratic republic. However imperfect a system it has been, the democratic republic has arguably done better than any other form of government in controlling the worst of humanity's ambitions. This cannot be overstated. So whatever evolves to replace the democratic republic should provide us with more mechanisms to check and channel those ambitions.

It's not a stretch to state that there is an authoritarian urge in all of us. For some of us it burns softly, as an ember. For others it can quickly be kindled into a fundamentalist fire. But not all ambition results in great evil. The democratic republic, more than any other form of government, has left room for the most ambitious to channel their desires to productive ends. So just as whatever system lies over the horizon should tamp down the will to power, it should ignite the spirits of entrepreneurship, innovation, and charity.

The End Is Nigh

"Democracy is the art and science of running the circus from the monkey cage," said H. L. Mencken. So what are we monkeys to do? We can get sucked into the ongoing reality show—the horse races, the scandals, and the controversies—with a bucketful of popcorn and a vague look of disgust. Or we can acknowledge the cage.

If we succumb to tribal tendencies, the bumper-sticker rationales, and the "I Voted" rectitude, we will perpetuate the whole charade. Each hanging chad will be a vote of complicity in this monstrous thing that has grown upon the backs of the people. At the very least, we can call this thing what it is: An illusion. Or we can be revolutionaries again. We can rattle the cage. A million little acts of civil disobedience here and there can add up fast.

I have done my best thus far, dear reader, to disabuse you of any unreflective faith in politics. At the least, I hope I've left you with some skepticism. My goal is not to criticize for criticism's sake. Instead I want to help people see good reasons not to cling too tightly to a system that might have outlived its usefulness.

When the time comes, you'll have good reasons to let go. Because politics as we know it is nigh at an end. In other words, even if you don't believe a word of this chapter, change is coming.

CHAPTER TWO

CRACKS IN THE PILLARS

Just as millions of anthozoan
polyps create, willy-nilly, a coral
reef, so do thousands upon
thousands of individual acts of
insubordination and evasion
create a political or economic
barrier reef of their own.
— James C. Scott[30]

IN 1977, reporter Carl Bernstein, of Watergate fame, wrote an exposé on his
fellow journalists. More than 400 of them, he revealed in *Rolling Stone*, had
done the business of the CIA. Members of the press had "provided a full range
of clandestine services—from simple intelligence gathering to serving as go-
betweens with spies in Communist countries." And in some cases, leaders of
top American news organizations had been in on it.[31]

Bernstein's exposé was just the start of what would become a larger picture of
collusion between US government agencies and the news media.

So much for objectivity—or the vision of the media as an independent check on
the federal government.

By 1979, a few other intrepid journalists began to lay bare the extent of the in-
cestuous relationship between the media and the CIA, much of which had apparently been covered up by the Church Committee in the wake of the Watergate hearings. The facts surrounding Operation Mockingbird,[32] for example,
demonstrated that the CIA had only to dangle a few carrots—and maybe brandish a couple of sticks—to co-opt the media for both intelligence and propa-

ganda purposes. And indeed, the media were very different animals in the 1950s. Massive. Top-down. Corporate.

Theories abound as to why this had been the case, but one of the most persuasive comes from serial entrepreneur and social theorist Jordan Greenhall, who posits that the media evolved this way. Greenhall thinks the organization of the media in the twentieth century was largely an emergent phenomenon. In other words, even if power was conspiring with the media, it was just the sort of conspiracy that had been likely to crop up at that place and time.

Greenhall calls it the "Blue Church." He says it "solves the problem of twentieth century social complexity through the use of mass media to generate manageable social coherence."

We might be skeptical of grand designs and conspiracy theories, but it's easy to notice that older people tend to be nostalgic about the Walter Cronkite[33] era. In those days, they say, we were more united. Barring a couple of instances like the Vietnam protests or the civil rights marches, our general civic narrative was, indeed, more coherent than it is today. And the older folks have a point, but for reasons that might now strike us as cynical.

"The conscious and intelligent manipulation of the organized habits and opinions of the masses is an important element in democratic society," wrote Edward Bernays in *Propaganda*.

> Those who manipulate this unseen mechanism of society constitute an invisible government which is the true ruling power of our country. . . . We are governed, our minds are molded, our tastes formed, our ideas suggested, largely by men we have never heard of. This is a logical result of the way in which our democratic society is organized. Vast numbers of human beings must cooperate in this manner if they are to live together as a smoothly functioning society.[34]

Though this should strike us as counter to the spirit of free expression and thought, Bernays was not exactly wrong.

The twentieth-century social order was built on a shared, centralized form of collective intelligence, according to Greenhall.

> The Blue Church is a kind of narrative/ideology control
> structure that is a natural result of mass media. It is an
> evolved (rather than designed) function that has come over
> the past half-century to be deeply connected with the
> Democratic political "Establishment" and lightly connected
> with the "Deep State" to form an effective political and
> dominant cultural force in the United States.

Greenhall believes we can trace the Blue Church's roots to the beginning of the
twentieth century, where it arose in response to "the new capabilities of mass
media for social control." By the early 1950s, the Blue Church began to play an
outsized role in shaping America's culture-producing institutions—and thus
public opinion. Sometime in the latter half of the twentieth century, it peaked.
But, writes Greenhall, "it is now beginning to unravel."[35]

In the twentieth century, society became much more complex. Information trav-
eled faster. And for people to see themselves in solidarity both with each other
and with a larger protective security apparatus, everyone would need to get the
right message. The Blue Church rationale had been: *our security requires both
a common enemy and a common narrative.*

And for the most part it worked. The only way to achieve a shared collective
intelligence, however, was to control the media. Power could no longer tolerate
the idea of the media as a loose collection of beat reporters getting scoops and
running with them on anyone's terms. Outlets, editors, reporters, and readers
would have to follow master narratives so that the people could socially cohere.

"The mass media serve as a system for communicating messages and symbols
to the general populace," wrote Noam Chomsky in his classic of media conspiracy, *Manufacturing Consent.* "It is their function to amuse, entertain, and in-
form, and to inculcate individuals with the values, beliefs, and codes of behavior that will integrate them into the institutional structures of the larger society."
Even if one is generally reluctant to agree with Chomsky, as I am reluctant, this
point is compelling.

Why is social coherence so important?

Greenhall reminds us that in the transition from the nineteenth to the twentieth
century, there were massive shifts in social complexity: agrarian to industrial,
rural to urban. Humanity leapt from horses to rail to cars and airplanes, effec-

tively shrinking the world. By 1953, Watson and Crick had identified the structure of DNA; Darwin had only published *On the Origin of Species* in 1859. The first theory of electromagnetism appeared in 1864, but by 1945, the first atomic bomb had been deployed. "This was a hell of a century."[36]

Human society cannot function "without a regulatory structure adequate to its level of complexity," according to Greenhall.[37] The Blue Church had been that regulatory structure, and therefore the emergent solution to the problem of maintaining social order in an increasingly complex world.

But then something happened: the Internet.

In the 1990s, hierarchical media organizations started to falter. A series of events began to reveal the cracks, and one might argue that the twentieth-century apparatus of collective intelligence began its decline sometime between dial-up modems and the election of Donald Trump.

The 2016 election was perhaps the first time the Blue Church media apparatus was in full-throated support of one politician and against another. And yet it failed. Hillary Clinton was a well-funded establishment politician running against a loutish outsider. According to Greenhall, however, Clinton's opponents executed a digital insurgency to ignite what he refers to as the "Red Religion," a populist movement with retrograde ideas and sophisticated communications tools. The Blue Church was neutralized. The media had fundamentally changed. Of course, there are all manner of distinct but interwoven causes of the 2016 election result. Nationalism. Scapegoating. Disaffection with the establishment. Hillary Clinton's lack of vision and charisma. Even though all of these were factors, Donald Trump would not have been elected without a digital insurgency capable of challenging the Blue Church. Old ideas. New tech.

Just one example lay with Cambridge Analytica. The big-data startup, fresh off an apparent win with Brexit, worked its magic with Trump, too. The modus operandi of Cambridge Analytica was to harvest sentiment data from social-media posts. They would then match this data against the most powerful of the personality models used by psychologists the world over: the Big Five. Finding the Big Five's patterns in the data, Cambridge Analytica could then mine for messages that the campaign could parrot back to those from whom it had been mined.

But Cambridge Analytica might be viewed as somewhat centralized. Memes from "Kekistan"—produced by the so-called "Autists of Kek"—were all about a clever mix of mockery and misinformation contra Clinton. Couple these Kekistani insurgents with foreign fake-news producers, and the result was a win for the famous billionaire who became beloved by both spit-and-sawdust America and those weary of Blue Church posturing.

One brilliant strategist predicted, if not seeded, the Red Religion insurgency in 2015. In a paper for NATO, Jeff Giesea wrote: "Memetic warfare can be useful at the grand narrative level, at the battle level, or in a special circumstance. It can be offensive, defensive, or predictive. It can be deployed independently or in conjunction with cyber, hybrid, or conventional efforts. The online battlefield of perception will only grow in importance in both warfare and diplomacy."[38]

Memetic warfare could be waged against ISIS or the Democratic National Committee.

Mainstream media as a mediating structure—a means of collective intelligence and social coherence—will never be the same. Decentralization means the popular control of making media yields agile platoons: citizen investigators, checkers, trolls, purveyors of fake news, and other dynamic new hive minds. These can assemble and dissolve in real time.

Think of the Gray Lady, a.k.a. the *New York Times*. Imagine her as a kind of automaton, powerful but stiff. She's surrounded by a thousand tiny drones. The drones are angry. The Gray Lady tries in vain to swat them with her cane. But her cane is no match for the swarm.

So what does this mean for social coherence?

It depends. Even if one thinks Greenhall is being too cynical in concluding that government and media were fated to collude in the twentieth century, one still might think the country needed some degree of social coherence. Social coherence is both a way of dealing with complexity and a way of maintaining some unity in the face of cultural entropy—diverse values, beliefs, and so on that can tend to fracture people. But social coherence for great secular religions, to preserve large, top-heavy nation states, might no longer be possible. (It might not be necessary, either.)

So in reckoning with the coming era, how do we get social coherence? We'll have to see. We can take heart in the fact that there is less at stake in the fate of any single system in decentralized environments with smaller jurisdictions than there is in the fate of a monolithic system. Decentralized environments are more "antifragile." Social coherence need only develop locally in most cases.

Whatever one thinks the future might or should be like, hierarchical media structures no longer provide social coherence. Knowledge and information no longer travel in bidirectional flows up and down chains of authority and expertise. The media have been lateralized. Information and disinformation alike want to be free. Social coherence will have to come about through different means, as within smaller units of social organization. The media are not the only mediating structure that is weakening. We have grown up with a few more pillars upon which civilization has depended, evolving more or less, since the time of Galileo.

In what follows, I have purposefully left out religion, though it most certainly belongs. Religion has served as a mediating structure for both morality and meaning, but I will leave it for another discussion. For now, suffice it to say the pillars that have supported civilization up to this point are showing cracks. Some will become obsolete. Others will change to the point that we can no longer recognize them.

The Firm

In 1931, a brilliant young man named Ronald Coase first presented his ideas about the firm in Dundee, Scotland, at the tender age of 21. His question: "Why and under what conditions should we expect firms to emerge?" Five years later, Coase published the seminal essay "The Nature of the Firm," in which he further develops that question, frames it, and answers it: Why isn't there a totally "free" market in labor? Or, more prosaically, why do organizations take on hierarchical forms?

Coase's answer was "transaction costs." The firm reduces the costs that would be incurred to continually coordinate actions among scattered people with disparate skill sets—all of whom would have to contract with one another and hammer out details of their contracts and then get themselves together somehow to divide labor and accomplish something profitable. So, up to a certain point, firms (organizations) arranged like hierarchies have been less costly to organize because it is usually cheaper for some people to give orders and some to take them, with the former paying the latter for the privilege.

But that's changing—and fast. It turns out that there are rules and tools reducing transaction costs. What we might call the "Coasian floor" is the level below which the costs of organization are cost prohibitive. And even though this book is certainly a paean to new rules and tools, here's something of a dirty secret: Clever people have been moving away from the hierarchical model without software assistance. That doesn't mean Coase is wrong. It means companies are evolving from the traditional top-down firm simply by changing their internal rules and thereby reducing transaction costs.

"People who work for businesses aren't treated the way businessmen themselves instinctively want to be treated," wrote philanthropist Richard Cornuelle in his 1975 book *De-managing America: The Final Revolution*. "They are told when to come to work, and often what to wear. They are guided by endless manuals. Their curiosity is stifled, their humanity diminished. As soon as their performance is subject to someone else's judgment, they become politicized. Their success is dependent on pressure and popularity."

One of the first businesspeople to innovate away from the hierarchical firm was Chris Rufer.[39] Morning Star Packing Company is a collection of tomato processing plants and tomato delivery trucks in California's Central Valley. In fact, the company processes so much tomato paste that if you eat spaghetti sauce or ketchup in the United States, there's a good chance you're eating Morning Star's product. The company is like a beating heart of tomato paste, pumping that stuff out in a massive vascular system—right onto your pasta.

One day, decades before Morning Star reached the size and scale it enjoys today, Rufer walked into his company and delivered the news: *There would be no more managers*. In fact, the Morning Star Packing Company would run on a new corporate operating system, originating in two simple rules: (1) don't threaten people; and (2) honor your commitments. Beyond that, everyone would be equal before those rules and no one would have any formal authority over any colleague. Even today, many executives would scoff at such a decision. But more than thirty years after Morning Star became self-managed, it was knocking at the door of $1 billion a year in revenues.

I asked Paul Green, Jr., a former Morning Star "colleague" (as everyone there is called), about his experiences there.

"At Morning Star, there are no titles; there's no structural hierarchy," said Green. "Each colleague comes into the enterprise with the same set of rights as any other. Colleagues commit to a personal commercial mission when they come aboard and, further, commit to what we call 'total responsibility'—essentially, they agree that they are totally responsible for the success of the entire enterprise."[40]

"That sounds heavy," I said.

Green continued by explaining that if people embrace personal responsibility for the whole company, they're more likely "to perform at the highest level" and to "find fulfillment in their careers." But this means giving people the freedom to act, which also means letting them take a risk and sometimes fail. And, according to Green, that means "everyone has the same authority in the enterprise with regards to acquiring resources (spending money), acquiring talent, and causing change. If the authority level is the same, then there's no real meaning to titles and artificial hierarchy."[41]

It's a company without bosses.

Fans of economist F. A. Hayek will recall the distinction between cosmos and taxis. *Cosmos* is unplanned, or "emergent," order. *Taxis* is planned order. According to Hayek, what distinguishes these two forms of order is that cosmos relies on agents operating within impartial rules. Taxis relies heavily on plans and commands. The punchline? Enterprises can be designed and managed, but economies cannot. Society is cosmos. A company is usually taxis.

An emergent order has no goals per se, just as a coral reef has no purpose. Only the people or organizations who make up the emergent order can or should have a purpose. And each purpose probably will be distinct from one person to the next, or from one organization to the next. Organizations do have purposes: *Sell luxury cars* might be one such purpose. *Help poor people find food and shelter* might be another.

So while a planned order might have a purpose, an emergent order cannot. Often, managers design organizations to carry out their purposes. They also carry out the planning and commanding—as a founder and CEO might very well plan and command with the purpose of putting shoes on people's feet. As Hayek rightly observed, people run into trouble when they try to assign some purpose to society, then proceed to plan as if the right sorts of people can implement that plan. Once you appreciate Hayek's distinction, it's easier to see why a central, Soviet-style planned economy doesn't work. And that's fine as far as it goes. Society self-organizes to a great extent. But what about companies? Must they always be planned?

If we thought cosmos and taxis were all there could be, it would seem cosmos is just the sum of all the designed organizations out there. But cosmos has a life of its own. What's as interesting, perhaps, is that some forms of organization have distinct *purposes*, but they don't use central plans, commands, or directives at all. They are neither cosmos nor taxis, but something in between. Let's call this kind of organization *esmos* or "swarm order." At companies like Morning Star, purpose and "command" are one and the same. For a "bare, abstract rule," the mission suffices. These new organizational forms are structured like neural networks or profitable hives.

Why hives? Despite unfortunate terms like "queen" and "worker," hives are actually distributed, nonhierarchical systems. For a swarm of insects, the mission might be "relocate the food source," which they carry out algorithmically through regurgitated food or pheromone secretions. But there are no managers, no directors, and no assignments from above. Planning, such as there is, is carried out in highly localized fashion by ad hoc teams operating according to their commitment to a mission.

When I pressed Green about operating in some sort of organizational anarchy, he replied: "I guess it is anarchy in the sense that there's no structural chain of command or hierarchy—no 'government' of sorts. But it would be a mistake to assume that it's disordered or without structure. On the contrary, it's very ordered and there is structure."

The difference in these organizations is how one arrives at order and structure. In traditional firms, it happens by design, that is, through some sort of command-and-control hierarchy. But at firms like Morning Star, groups of individuals create order through social networks built around circumstances and needs.

It's as if the firm had an invisible hand.

In a post about decentralized organizations, economist Yanis Varoufakis writes that "Hayek's argument that markets protect us from serfdom (i.e. from authoritarian hierarchies) is weakened substantially by the fact that he has precious little to say about corporate serfdom." After all, millions of people must submit to hierarchies like those in Walmart or Microsoft "in order to make a living or to get a chance to unfold their talents."[42]

Varoufakis has a point, well, up to a point. Happily, more companies are seeing the value of transitioning away from hierarchy. And in fact, it's not just that companies are forming their own self-management styles. Successful consulting firms are now devoted to helping companies make the transition.

Enter Brian Robertson.

Robertson is founder of a management philosophy called "holacracy." Robertson travels the world showing companies how to operate without bosses (and bizarrely, those bosses pay him to do so). The consequence is a form of organization that runs decidedly more like an organism. Managers can instead be visionaries. Workers are more autonomous. Everyone is accountable to the mission. One gets the impression this bald, animated man is something of a closet anarchist. "Holacracy," writes Robertson,

> takes some of the organizational design functions that traditionally reside with a CEO or executive team and places them into *processes* that are enacted throughout an organization, with everyone's participation. This governance process distributes authority and clarifies expectations throughout the organization, and is driven by those doing its work and sensing tensions along the way. . . . Governance generates organizational clarity, then continually evolves it to integrate the team's latest learnings and fit its changing realities.[43]

Such a system enables organizations to situate decision-making power in the hands of people with certain capabilities within certain roles. These roles are arranged within the wider corpus like organs. The whole ends up being greater than the sum of parts. As a bonus, employees tend to be happier, because they are freer and, paradoxically, more collaborative.

But all this decentralization is decidedly different from the way most of us think about a company.

The dominant metaphor for the Industrial Age was the machine. Any of the following sound familiar?

+ "Our company's a well-oiled machine."
+ "We need to jump-start sales."
+ "I'm just a cog."
+ "This is our blueprint for success."
+ "We need to tinker with the business model."

And it's no wonder: Most companies were set up to produce goods with machines. So, when we thought about how to arrange a company, the machine
metaphor animated our thinking.

One whose thinking had been so animated was Frederick Winslow Taylor. His
Principles of Scientific Management shaped the dominant form of business organization. And to give credit where it's due, Taylor's vision of the firm resulted in a productivity revolution relative to what had come before. But it also
broke a lot of spirits.

Human beings were treated as moveable cogs that managers assembled in productive ways. Life was hard. And Karl Marx, wrong as he'd been about a lot of
things, was right about what division of labor had done to workers. Taylorite
management added to the alienation.

The four basic rules of Taylor's scientific management were:

1. Develop scientific methods for doing work.
2. Establish goals for productivity.
3. Establish systems of rewards for meeting the goals.
4. Train the personnel in how to use the methods and thereby meet the goals.

In some sense these should strike us as fairly unobjectionable rules. People still
use them, after all, and in some sense we shouldn't throw out the proverbial
baby.

But the assumptions upon which these rules are based—and the potentially
good rules this set leaves out—reinforce the classic corporate form with its
well-known command-and-control structure. Executive. Upper management.
Middle management. Staff. There are variations, but this is more or less a description of the twentieth-century firm. And it's no accident. In fact, we can't
blame Taylorite management philosophy entirely for the corporate form, despite the fact that practitioners tend to treat employees like cogs instead of people. But Taylor's approach seems to begin and end with monetary rewards.

In a complex society, employees have to be motivated to work beyond basic tasks. And that takes more than money. According to Daniel Pink, it takes:

- **Autonomy:** People want to be self-directed. Autonomous employees tend to be more engaged than merely compliant ones.
- **Mastery:** People want to get better skills. Employees who do feel they are growing as professionals.
- **Purpose:** People want to do something that has meaning and is important. Businesses that only focus on profits without valuing purpose will end up with poor customer service and unhappy employees.

If we start looking for ways to let orders emerge within our organizations, people may see what's possible without formal authorities and central planners— and they may like what they see. What they see could surprise them.

"The desire for fully-specified, legalistic, control-oriented regulation leads to this type of primitive, planned order,"[44] says economist Lynne Kiesling. Such a primitive form of organization does not just take its toll on the potential value achievable through open collaboration. But in strictly planned orders, "minds wither and atrophy, increasing the primitive and simplistic nature of the resulting order."

Essentially, in command-and-control organizations you get wasted potential. People operating in the rank and file have to navigate between the Scylla of blind obedience and the Charybdis of insubordination. On the other hand, writes Kiesling, rules that allow for increased creativity and knowledge make for far more robust organizations, allowing us to operate in environments that are complex beyond our understanding. "Thus," writes Kiesling, "relinquishing the base desire to control and manage is crucial to well-being, growth, and living together in civil society."[45]

I think most of us agree we want well-being, growth, and a civil society. So now the question becomes: How do we achieve them?

Internally, companies can experiment with different forms of self-management, which tend to be less dehumanizing. Distributed autonomous organizations and other tech-enabled forms of organization are coming online, too. Once executives begin to see the power of decentralization inside their organizations, the big lessons of the extended order may follow. In other words, we can start by implementing good rules and being less autocratic in our own businesses; society as a whole will profit.

Science

Science is undergoing a wrenching evolutionary change.

Most of us do not realize that what is carried out in the name of science is dubious at best, flat wrong at worst. It appears we're putting too much faith in science—particularly the kind of science that relies on expert opinion.

In fact, experts making social-science prognostications turned out to be mostly wrong, according to political science writer Philip Tetlock's decades-long review[46] of expert forecasts. And in a Center for Open Science meta-study led by a University of Virginia professor,[47] the results of more than half of one hundred psychology studies tested could not be reproduced.

Since the time of bloodletting, there has been perhaps no more egregious example of bad expert advice than in the area of health and nutrition. For most of our lives, we've been taught some variation on the US Department of Agriculture food pyramid.[48] The advice: Eat mostly breads and cereals, then fruits and vegetables, and very little fat and protein. Do so and you'll be thinner and healthier. Animal fat and butter are unhealthy. Certain carbohydrate-rich foods are good for you, as long as they are whole grain.

Most of us aligned our understanding about food to that idea.

"Measures used to lower the plasma lipids in patients with hyperlipidemia will lead to reductions in new events of coronary heart disease," claimed the National Institutes of Health in 1971. The so-called "lipid theory" had the support of the US Surgeon General. Most doctors fell in line behind the advice. Saturated fats like butter and bacon became public enemy number one. People flocked to the supermarket to buy "heart-healthy" margarines. And yet Americans were getting fatter.

But early in the twenty-first century something interesting happened: people began to go against the grain (no pun intended), and they started talking about their small experiments eating saturated fat. By 2010, the lipid theory—not to mention the USDA food pyramid—was dead. Forty years of nutrition orthodoxy had been upended. Now the same experts are joining the chorus from the rear.[49]

But the problem doesn't just affect nutrition. Recall in chapter 1 we touched on the problem of peer review and "a paucity of attempts at experimental replication."[50]

Richard Horton, editor of the British medical journal *The Lancet*, writes that the "case against science is straightforward: much of the scientific literature, perhaps half, may simply be untrue."[51] And according to Julia Belluz and Steven Hoffman, another review found that researchers at Amgen were unable to reproduce 89 percent of landmark cancer research findings for potential drug targets.[52] Contrast the questionable progress of science in these areas with that of applied sciences such as computer science and engineering, where use cases and market feedback mechanisms help to weed out false claims. It's the difference between Murphy's Law and Moore's Law.

So what's happening?

Three major catalysts account for the current upheaval in the sciences. First, a few intrepid experts have started looking around to see whether studies in their respective fields are holding up. Second, competition among scientists to grab headlines is becoming more intense. Third, informal networks of amateur checkers have started questioning expert opinion and talking to each other. And the likely real action is in this third catalyst, as the paleo-diet movement makes clear. Amateur checkers subject scientific claims to a kind of evolutionary pressure. Currently, the cost of checking science is going down, and the price of being wrong is going up.

But let's be abundantly clear: the unsexy world of checking scientific reproducibility needed advocates, too, as the case of the Reproducibility Project makes clear.

Experts don't like having their expertise checked and rechecked, because their dogmas get called into question. When dogmas are challenged, fame, funding, and cushy jobs are at stake. Most will fight tooth and nail to stay on the gravy train, which can translate into coming under the sway of certain biases. It could mean they're more likely to cherry-pick their data, exaggerate their results, or ignore counterexamples. Far more rarely, it can mean they're motivated to engage in outright fraud.[53]

Not all of the fault for scientific error lies with scientists, per se. Some of it lies with methodologies and assumptions most of us have taken for granted for years. Social and research scientists have far too much faith in data aggregation, a process that can conceal the important circumstances of time and place. Many researchers make inappropriate inferences and predictions based on a narrow band of observed data points that are plucked from wider phenomena in a complex system. And, of course, some scientists are notoriously good at getting statistics to paint a picture that looks a lot like their pet theories.

Matters worsen when disciplines produce their own holy scriptures. Psychiatry's *Diagnostic and Statistical Manual* or *DSM* is one such bible. These guidelines, when married with government funding, lobbyist influence, or insurance payouts, have the tendency to protect incomes and institutional practices. It's no wonder that changes in diagnostic criteria to the *DSM* over the years have correlated with political realities about how psychiatrists get paid and by whom.

But perhaps the most significant methodological problem with science is over-reliance on the peer-review process. Peer review can perpetuate groupthink, the cartelization of knowledge, and the compounding of biases. That's because peer review amounts to a game of elite back-scratching. In fact, according to Asit K. Biswas and Julian Kirchherr, "an average academic journal article is read in its entirety by about 10 people."[54] Another 2007 estimate claimed that half of all academic journal articles are only read by the editors who publish them.[55]

But it's not just that it's wasteful. The problem with expert opinion is that it is often cloistered and restrictive. When science starts to seem like a walled system built around a small group of elites, many of whom are only sharing ideas with each other, hubris can take hold. No amount of training or smarts can keep up with an expansive network of outsiders who have a bigger stake in finding the truth than in shoring up the walls of a guild.

It's true that to some degree, we have to rely on experts and scientists. It's a perfectly natural part of specialization and division of labor that some people will know more about certain things than you, and that you are likely to need their help at some point. (I try to stay away from accounting; I am probably not proficient at brain surgery, either.) But that doesn't mean that we shouldn't question authority, even when authorities know more about their field than we do.

"Toward the end of the nineteenth century, the center of intellectual discourse moved from the city to the University," wrote Cornuelle, "and at about the same time, social inquiry became disintegrated, fragmented, professionalized, institutionalized. Throughout the twentieth century, with a few predictable and isolated exceptions, social thought has become more and more sterile, scientistic, and irrelevant." To a great degree it remains so. But "social thought must be reintegrated, de-secularized, de-institutionalized, and reconnected to the life of the society."[56] This process has begun.

When you get an army of networked people—sometimes amateurs—thinking, talking, tinkering, and toying with ideas—you can hasten a paradigm shift. And this is exactly what we are witnessing. It's becoming harder for experts to count on the obscurity of their disciplines to keep power. But it's in cross-disciplinary pollination of the network that many different good ideas can sprout and be tested.

The best thing that can happen to science is for it to open itself up to everyone, even people who are not credentialed experts, then let the checkers start to talk to each other. Leaders, influencers, and force multipliers will emerge. You might think of them as communications hubs or bigger nodes in a network. Some will be cranks and hacks. But the best will win out, and the cranks will be worked out of the system in time.

A network might include a million amateurs willing to give a pair of eyes or a different perspective. Most in this army of experimenters get results and share their experiences with others in the network. What follows is a wisdom-of-crowds phenomenon. Millions of people not only share results, but challenge the orthodoxy.

"Can a citizen scientist win a Nobel Prize?" asks uBiome CEO Jessica Richman. "The technological forces that are globalizing and integrating all of us are increasingly bringing us together to do science. . . . What will the world look like when you, me and everyone . . . can contribute to this great enterprise of science?"

In his legendary 1962 essay, "The Republic of Science," scientist and philosopher Michael Polanyi wrote the following passage, which beautifully illustrates the problems of science and of society, and it explains how they will be solved in the peer-to-peer age:

> Imagine that we are given the pieces of a very large jigsaw puzzle, and suppose that for some reason it is important that our giant puzzle be put together in the shortest possible time. We would naturally try to speed this up by engaging a number of helpers; the question is in what manner these could be best employed.[57]

Polanyi states you could progress through multiple parallel-but-individual processes. But the way to cooperate more effectively is to let them work on solving the puzzle in sight of the others so that every time a piece of it is fitted in by one helper, the others will immediately watch out for the next potential step. Under this system, each helper will act on his own initiative by responding to the latest achievements of the others, and the completion of their joint task will be greatly accelerated. We have here in a nutshell the way in which a series of independent initiatives are organized to a joint achievement by mutually adjusting themselves at every successive stage to the situation created by others who are acting likewise.

Just imagine if Polanyi had lived to see the Internet.

This process is the Republic of Science. Collaboration is how smart people with different interests and skill sets can help put together life's great puzzles. In the Republic of Science, there is certainly room for experts. But they are hubs among nodes. And in this network, leadership is earned not by sitting atop an institutional hierarchy with the plumage of a tenured professor, but by contributing, experimenting, communicating, and learning with the rest of a larger hive mind. This is science in the peer-to-peer age.

Recall that above I mentioned that the Internet itself had set the stage for a new form of collective intelligence that did not fit neatly into the previous paradigm, the Blue Church. New media insurgencies caused much of the Blue Church to unravel. As it happens, the Blue Church is not just a media and academic structure. According to Greenhall, it still controls much of science, but

> the world is just too big and moving too fast for this kind of control hierarchy to keep up—even when it is trying to do its best, it is going to get in the way. Addressing [global] challenges is going to require the innovation of an entirely new approach to how we collectively make sense of and act in the world.[58]

If science's Blue Church is already obsolete, think of the structures on whose behalf the Blue Church speaks. One of the first signs that the social singularity is near is that our sense-making apparatus is evolving. *Scientia potestas est.* And if that old truism about knowledge being power has any substance, what will that power do when the people have it?

Education

Chairs and desks are arranged in rows. Before the class is a chalkboard or whiteboard. Bells ring periodically throughout the day; students file in and file out like cattle. In between the bells they sit, some fidgeting. A teacher ladles out information from a textbook. Because the curriculum in that textbook is standardized and approved by central authorities, deviation from said curriculum would harm test scores. Bad test scores could affect the teacher's performance evaluations. So teachers—to the extent they are accountable for performance—have incentives to teach from a standardized curriculum.

The students continue to fidget. Some are bored and disconnected, others are distracted. A few figure out how to press the lever to get the pellet. Maybe there are a few opportunities for some of them to engage and challenge the text, but this takes a back seat to simply getting through it all. The teacher, sapped of creativity and drive, looks bored too. The most familiar part of the cycle is that Pavlovian bell, whose only reward is a break from fifty minutes of monotony.

"I've noticed a fascinating phenomenon in my thirty years of teaching," writes venerable teacher and iconoclast John Taylor Gatto in *Dumbing Us Down.* "Schools and schooling are increasingly irrelevant to the great enterprises of the planet. No one believes anymore that scientists are trained in science classes or politicians in civics classes or poets in English classes. The truth is that schools don't really teach anything except how to obey orders."[59]

Taylor thinks that although today's teachers are caring and hardworking, "the institution is psychopathic—it has no conscience. It rings a bell and the young man in the middle of writing a poem must close his notebook and move to a different cell where he must memorize that humans and monkeys derive from a common ancestor."

So this entire education model has been compared to a Soviet-era factory. In such a factory, there was no price system, no feedback mechanism, no creativity or entrepreneurial spirit. Central planners estimated what the people needed and doled it out. If you needed shoes, there were three sizes. If you needed a coat, there were three sizes. If you needed meat, there were three kinds (in the lean times, "tongue, offal and scraps").[60]

Analogously, in centralized education, students are viewed as outputs, their heads like buckets to be filled with information curated by central elites. After twelve years, if they are to be "prepared for college," they will have memorized as much of the curriculum as possible. The students' incentives, then—to the extent they align with curriculum developers' goals—are to consume and regurgitate.

The bright ones don't really learn much from these schemes, certainly not critical thinking or creativity. Instead they explore online after school lets out. Perhaps they find time to read something compelling before bedtime. The rest, if they don't drop out, muddle through till graduation. At this point they must quickly figure out the ways of the world, a world that does not provide either the thick chowder of the free-lunch line or the thin gruel of standardization.

Higher education is little better. A mix of student-loan debt, vanity-based alumni endowment funds, and government subsidy shores up a great guild. So if the primary and secondary education system looks mostly like a state-run monopoly, higher education has the qualities of a cartel. The result is that these mediating structures seem to be frozen in amber. The systems have persisted for more than a century due largely to their resistance to change and to tight control over the flow channels that keep them alive. And as with any other monopoly, guild, or cartel, benefits accrue to members. Threaten those members and you're accused of threatening to take education from children.

Monopolies, guilds, cartels, and organizations that resemble them fight fiercely to protect their interests. In higher education, there are differences between public and private universities. But all share the basic guild structure:

- **Accreditation Boards:** Protective oligopolies that give members (universities) a degree of security from competition through bestowing the power to grant degrees.
- **Universities:** Protective guilds that give their members (instructors) the power to give grades (which students need to get degrees).
- **Students:** A protected group that spends time and money on the guild to be granted degrees—that is, signaling mechanisms for professional life or graduate school.

Advantages accrue to these groups by virtue of the structure. When one adds heavy subsidies like federal student loans and Pell grants, it can make the system sclerotic. Malaise and inflation set in. Alumni donors go on blindly throwing money at these hoary guilds. Taxpayers think they're supporting education instead of bureaucratic bloat. And students think that sociology degree is going to set them up with a good job.

Of course, the Blue Church rears its head again. Jordan Greenhall writes of academia that

> the students are the audience. Their job is to pay attention to the credentialed authority. To listen and watch closely and to learn from the professor the nature of "good opinion" in this particular domain. If they do a good job in this, that is, if they can answer questions correctly according to the authorities' evaluation process, then they pass. If not, they fail.[61]

Greenhall thinks that while the content matters, it's the form that really matters because, whatever the subject, "every class is a lesson in how to play the Blue Church game."

Then, of course, cartelization via accreditation allows universities to gain these advantages in anticompetitive ways. Shielded from market dynamics, political entrepreneurship allows education bureaucrats to cartelize without much fear of customer defection. In primary and secondary education, people simply are forced to pay for a failing system offered for "free."

In an entrepreneurial market, there are strong incentives for one to defect from a cartel by lowering prices and increasing quality or output. But if cartels are propped up by significant cost shifting, as they are in education by, for example, subsidies, student loans, accreditation, tenure, and union agitation, incentives to defect from the cartel evaporate. Any existing organization has developed secure channels through which favors from the political class and mostly ignorant taxpayers continue to flow; system-wide reform would require wholesale institutional change. That would mean big changes to the rules. Those who bear the costs—taxpayers, parents, and some students—are at a disadvantage compared to well-paid interests closer to the action.

But change is coming.

Despite resistance from vocal beneficiaries of the status quo, subversive inno-vators are in the process of creating an antidote. It doesn't help that most be-lieve public schooling is a sort of panacea, that is, if we just keep pouring money into it. It also doesn't help that many people think a conventional uni-versity degree is the primary key to success in life. Both of these mass halluci-nations are holding us back. And the only way to dispel the illusion is to criti-cize by creating.

Primary, secondary and higher education are all ripe for disruption. And the dis-ruption has begun:

* Serial school founder Michael Strong has started seven schools in his ca-reer so far. And as an educational entrepreneur, Strong has been actively hostile to the standardization regime. In fact, thinks Strong, the best way to teach is to have a conversation. "I have led Socratic discussions in liter-ally hundreds of classrooms around the world," said Strong. "I can go into any school anywhere and, given enough time, transform a group of young people who are resistant to learning into a group that is passionate about learning, with significant measurable results on the SAT verbal exam."[62] Paradoxically, then, Strong's Socratic techniques help students navigate standardized tests better than teaching to the test.
* Educational entrepreneur Isaac Morehouse founded Praxis in 2013. Praxis is a program for bright college-age students who, instead of college, work in paid apprenticeships while engaging in cutting-edge curricula. Instead of leaving the program $30,000 in debt (at least), most leave the program with $30,000-a-year jobs (at least). As of this writing, Praxis boasts a graduation rate of 96 percent, with graduates earning $50,000 per year on average.
* School franchiser Robert Luddy has created a model for both primary and secondary education. Tuition at one of Luddy's private schools costs only $500-$600 per month. No frills. No football stadiums. Just quality educa-tion at a low price in a classic case of "disruptive innovation" *a la* Clayton Christensen.
* Jason King, an entrepreneur known for helping homeless people adopt Bitcoin and find shelter in a community forest, in 2018 launched the Acad-emy School of Blockchain in response to the high demand for developers. Academy is an accredited (but distributed) post-secondary school whose unique structure allows students to connect directly with employers upon completion of the program. Students from all over the world participate.

These are but a handful of examples, but they suggest alternatives that could catch fire.

Venture capitalist Laura Deming was only 23 when she closed her second round of funding for an antiaging venture capital outfit called the Longevity Fund. Preoccupied with aging and biology since she was a girl, she grew up an autodidact. Her parents unschooled her until she went off to MIT at 14; then, after a year, she dropped out to take a Thiel Fellowship, which is for young people who leave college to start ventures. I asked Laura's dad, John, about his educational philosophy as a parent.

"Every human is born with a unique set of general aptitudes," John Deming said. "Play with, poke, observe your kids to discover those. Hang with them. Have fun with them. Live on their level. Explain everything to them from a scientific point of view."

In the elder Deming's responses, I sensed that the genetic dice might have been loaded in his daughter's favor. But then I also sensed it takes a good parent to ensure good genes get fully expressed.

"A kid is born with an innate, very powerful logical operator but they do not have much context. So they can learn math. I got Laura Saxon home-study math books," he said. "She worked through first-year university calculus by age 11. I didn't have to check the test, all of which she completed. Why would a self-learning kid cheat on exams? Humans are also born with an innate narrative receptor. So in addition to math, I gave the stories, mainly biographies of major innovators and achievers, which are far more exciting than most fiction."

John admits one of the simplest lessons he tried to impart is that the key to a good life is making good choices. That must have sunk in because one day Laura asked her dad: "Can you tell me how to make good choices?"

"No," said John to the young Laura. "You just start making your own choices and you'll learn to make better choices. Per Euclid, there's no royal road to geometry. I'll make sure you don't die or become permanently crippled."

It turned out John's philosophy had been simple: Don't force anything. Feed their curiosity and let them follow it wherever it leads.

Notice that most of the preceding examples don't feature technology. Subtle changes away from the centralized-education model are enough to start the process. People care more about their kids than some abstract sense of civic duty, so defection from public education will approach a tipping point. Technology will simply accelerate the process. And as alternatives become better, faster and cheaper, people will have greater incentives to defect.

So the question remains: How can technological decentralization help catalyze education reform? This pillar will be one of the toughest to crack, simply because children need to be looked after while parents are working. This reality makes the child-warehousing model of education difficult to dislodge, especially in the era of two-income households. Not everyone can homeschool. Still, some promising trends recommend themselves.

First, blended learning—the hybridization of ed tech and traditional pedagogy—is already an option for parents with flexible schedules. As new models develop, people will seek the right balance of project-based learning, self-directed learning, and traditional teaching.

Second, education co-ops are becoming increasingly popular. These are being made even more robust by parents who can participate actively, even if that participation is limited to one day per week.

Third, gales of creative destruction will be unleashed by connectivity, competition, and cryptography. Smart contracts will enable students to complete assignments in their own time and customize curricula—all while receiving credit or badges for each course component completed. Young people will also make their own decks and portfolios, if not launch their own microventures.

Of course, no one can truly predict the future. But failure to improve is almost always limited by a failure of imagination. Here's a vision from the Institute for the Future:

> Welcome to the year 2026, where strange and surprising things are happening . . .
>
> ♦ Anyone can use the Ledger to teach or mentor anyone else. (And get paid for it.) In fact, you can pay down your student loans by teaching forward what you learned in school.

- You can get credit for learning that happens anywhere, not just in schools or formal classes. The Ledger will also track skills you build just doing what you love, or spending time with friends and family.
- Employers can match you with projects and gigs that perfectly fit the level of learning you have right now. There's no need to finish school to have a thriving career.
- When you master a new skill at work, that goes on your learning record, too.
- You have a complete record of how much income each skill or lesson you've learned has helped you generate —so you know the exact value of every part of your education.
- Investors can help pay for your education. In return, they get a percentage of your future earnings tied to the skills they paid you to learn. This fuels a new speculative economy as people invest in building a workforce for what they hope will be the most lucrative skills.

Could a future like this really happen? It's already happening.[63]

Now all that's left to figure out is who will look after the kids while the parents are at work.

Money and Finance

Since the time of ancient empires, currency has been the lifeblood of an economy and an instrument of power for the political class. Where in the United States the Fed has printed, the Romans had minted. The consequence has each time been the same: the money supply gets manipulated and debased.

Emperor Augustus, for example, created a central coin system in Rome that became the master currency. But Augustus flooded the empire with too many coins, according to historian Max Shapiro, who wrote that "the volume of money he (Augustus) issued in the three decades between 27 BC and 6 AD was more than ten times the amount issued by his predecessors in the twenty years before."[64] Of course, prices soared for the average Roman. To make matters worse, successive emperors diluted the amount of gold and silver in the coins, until by 341 CE, Emperor Constans I diminished the nummus (monetary unit) to only 0.4 percent silver and 196 coins per pound. The monetary system had long been collapsed, and inflation continued to spiral out of control for generations, causing poverty and decline. Many Romans voted with their feet, moving to other countries.[65]

In the United States parallels to Rome abound: Bread and circuses plus monetary manipulation. And the decline in currency's purchasing power is happening here, too. Because inflation is a result of too much money chasing too few goods, we have to put most of the blame at the feet of the Federal Reserve—a mysterious, quasi-private megabank charged with determining how much money is in circulation and keeping it stable.

In the short timeline of monetary policy in the twentieth century, the buying power of the US dollar has decreased by 97 percent. Experts use all manner of justifications for why this is the best of possible worlds. The Federal Reserve states it wants to control inflation, but it also manipulates the price of credit. And because the US dollar has been divorced from the gold and silver standards, it has become easier simply to print money, whether for the purposes of monetary "stimulus" or, as some say, to benefit cronies on Wall Street. There has been scant incentive to save and too many incentives to spend.

In the wake of the 2007 and 2008 financial crises, a group of subversive software developers had had enough. Indeed, in Bitcoin's genesis block, in the first ever recording of a fact on the Bitcoin blockchain, someone coded a *London Times* headline from January 3, 2009: "Chancellor on Brink of Second Bailout for Banks." We don't know who the pseudonymous Satoshi Nakamoto is, but we do know that he (or they) must have been closely associated with a group of legal theorists, cryptographers, and cypherpunks that includes Hal Finney, Wei Dai, and Nick Szabo. For all we know, one or all of these could have been Satoshi Nakamoto. And in 2008, Nakamoto presented the Bitcoin white paper[66] to the world.

It contained multitudes.

First, Nakamoto described a system of public and private keys, which allowed parties to transact. But in order to prevent double spending, there had to be a way to time-stamp the event and ensure its fidelity system wide. Collections of time-stamped items were known as blocks, and these blocks would form a chain—event by event—known by all. This came to be known as the blockchain. Add a few more layers of computer science and cryptography and a verification system known as "proof of work," and the world had the specs for the world's first digital currency.

I hope you'll forgive the limited technical description, above. But the big idea here is that suddenly the world could imagine digital technology that allowed for the simultaneous recording, replication, and global sharing of data across people and devices—in the case of Bitcoin, transaction data. Because there would be no central warehousing of the data, it would be nearly impossible to alter, censor or fabricate. And in Bitcoin, the concept of the distributed ledger was given expression.

But it wasn't just a way of transmitting and receiving digital funds. The entire transaction network was designed to resist interference by providing a path between two parties that left out central banks and financial intermediaries. The idea of the smart contract lay in waiting, too, but let us not get ahead of ourselves.

The amazing thing that had been unleashed onto the world was a cryptocurrency with extraordinary properties, including a way to:

- store resources securely;
- transmit resources anywhere, anytime;
- avoid intermediaries such as central banks; and
- avoid manipulation such as currency inflation.

Bitcoin allowed people the world over to avoid the storage and security costs of gold, the devaluation of currency, and the general reliance on financial institutions that cannot always be trusted.

As of this writing, it is not clear whether any or all of the forks of (variations on) Bitcoin will survive. It's also not clear whether which of the so-called "altcoins" will make it in the evolutionary ecosystem that is the market, perhaps to topple the various Bitcoins. What is clear, though, is that the genie is out of the bottle.

Cryptocurrency properties will have to match human wants and needs. Indeed, most cryptocurrencies are currently deflationary—meaning one can't simply create more of them. As more people acquire these currencies, their purchasing power goes up, not down. Over time, though, rapid adoption resembles an S curve, which is to say we're likely to see prices for cryptocurrencies stabilize once they penetrate the global market.

But even as cryptocurrencies appreciate in value in their uptake phase, more and more people will prefer them to fiat currencies, because fiat currencies lose value (purchasing power) over time. The upshot of this is that rapid adoption of cryptocurrencies could mean the weakening, or even the end, of some central banking systems. People may simply not need them.

Cryptocurrencies amount to the realization of F. A. Hayek's vision for competing private currencies—only more decentralized. Hayek advocated a system of private currency in which financial institutions created currencies that competed for adoption by the masses. According to Hayek,

> this would mean in the first instance the abolition of any kind of exchange control or regulation of the movement of money between these countries, as well as the full freedom to use any of the currencies for contracts and accounting. Further, it would mean the opportunity for any bank located in these countries to open branches in any other on the same terms as established banks.[67]

Hayek could not have anticipated technologies that would obviate the need for banks. Nor did he consider that international currency movement would be carried out not by law but by network design, and that distributed-ledger accounting would be transparent and automatic to everyone.

To Hayek, stability was the minimum decisive factor for adoption—a test that some fiat currencies (currencies issued by governments and not backed by something valuable, such as gold or silver) can pass to varying degrees. And, indeed, central banks generally manipulate currency to maintain that stability. According to the Federal Reserve Bank of San Francisco, "Monetary policy has two basic goals: to promote 'maximum' sustainable output and employment and to promote 'stable' prices."[68] In other words, even though the dollar generally loses purchasing power over time, you can still go to the store and buy your milk for four dollars per jug and return six months later to find it at a similar price.

Hayek argued that competition would favor currencies with the greatest stability because a depreciating currency hurts creditors and an appreciating currency
hurts debtors. Users would choose currencies they expect to provide an acceptable intersection—that is, relative stability. Hayek suggested experimentation
would likely lead to a basket of commodities forming a more-or-less ideal monetary base. "Institutions" would issue and regulate their currency primarily
through loan making and secondarily through buying and selling currency.
What the modern market in cryptocurrencies shows us, however, is that people
want lots of different things.

Employment and price stability are thus not the only values. People also want
purchasing power and financial sovereignty. The upgrade with cryptocurrencies
is not just that there is no longer a need for financial institutions to mediate, or
for the experimentation described above, but that everything Hayek described
could someday be fully decentralized. Manipulation by central banks goes
away. Risks associated with panics and banks' dual role as lending institutions
go away. Even the transaction costs of Bitcoin mining and scaling problems
would lead to the evolution of Bitcoin, as well as innovations by competitors.

Some will want price stability. Others will be OK with deflation. Cryptography
helps confer individual agency so that ordinary people can be the judge of what
they want out of their money. As of this writing, however, the adoption of cryptocurrency by the general public faces a lot of barriers, many having to do with
a lack of simplicity or security. But most of these obstacles are kinks to be
worked out by armies of developers. When we consider that the global economy could eventually run on cryptocurrencies, the implications are staggering.

Early Bitcoin expert Daniel Krawisz describes a process he dubs "hyperbitcoinization,"[69] in which a cryptocurrency overtakes a fiat currency through voluntary adoption by the many.

> As the government forms a habit of inflating the money
> supply, its people form a habit of anticipating rising prices.
> This prevents the government from gaining as much each
> time it inflates. Thus, to get the same kick, the government
> must inflate more. The money loses value once people an-
> ticipate such heavy inflation that they can't spend it fast
> enough and it no longer functions as a currency.[70]

Krawisz goes on to explain that hyperinflation is a consequence of central banks' continuous interventions, which prevent normal monetary equilibria. In order to stay ahead of citizens, the "government must continually alter its own behavior," but as soon as the people start to anticipate the government's policies, "the government must change the policy by increasing the rate of inflation."[71]

Today, people can simply escape inflation by adopting a cryptocurrency.

Hyperbitcoinization, then, is a "transition from an inferior currency to a superior one," and its adoption is simply a series of arbitrage events that were never possible before. A single monetary monopoly can no longer game the system.

Software developer Justin Goro puts the matter forcefully: "The current ambient state dines at the table of central banking legitimacy but bitcoin has come to kick the legs out. The first and most obvious victory bitcoin won over the central banking cartel was to expose and eliminate inflation."[72] The choice to accept inflation, "an omnipresent mechanism of theft," is now a personal choice. Just a decade or so ago, inflation was thought to be like gravity.[73]

What if these prognosticators are right? Many will lament the loss of central banking, parasitic as the nation-state has become on its existence. Many more will lament the loss of the bread and circuses that flow from an omnipresent taxing authority.

Here's Justin Goro again:

> The next ambient institution to fall will be the state's asserted ownership of all matters finance. This one gives it legitimate authority to tax our income. In recent times, states have begun agitating that profits made in bitcoin would be subject to tax. This attempt to tax cryptoflows radically reduces the scope of use cases open to the nascent industry.[74]

But this is the thing about all things crypto. In one sense, it's rather like a balloon in that if you squeeze it on one end, it expands somewhere else. One can see the crypto markets migrate around the world as regulators in China or the US attempt to squeeze.

In another sense, it's like an evolving organism, in that if you try to kill it, it will adapt to become stronger, smarter, or more subversive—whether that happens through "obfuscating technologies" that will "continue to conceal flows between wallets"[75] or through international smart contracts that change the rules by which people live without the permission of authorities.

But aside from death, Benjamin Franklin told us, the only thing in life we could count on is taxes. So what does that mean for cryptocurrency? "Make no mistake," Goro warns, "cryptocurrency and income tax cannot coexist. The ambient state can choose to either pivot to property taxes or see their revenues eventually vanish. Cryptocurrency tax evasion is an anti-fragile beast which means that the more the state clamps down, the better the evasive technology will get."[76]

At this point, dear reader, you might be worried that this transition can only yield dire outcomes. We should expect such a response, as the nation state has been the All-father and All-mother of the people for generations.

Those who would adopt cryptocurrencies might appear to be selfish tax evaders, then, abandoning their responsibilities to their fellows and to the public benefits that accrue. And indeed a kind of mass loss aversion could provide justification for authorities to become far more totalitarian in response.

But for now, let's just make a bold claim: humanity will adapt to these new circumstances and, working together, we will become our own social safety net.[77]

CHAPTER THREE

THE SOCIAL SINGULARITY IS NEAR

We don't much care if you don't approve of the software we write. We know that software can't be destroyed and that a widely dispersed system can't be shut down.

—Eric Hughes[78]

EVERY INNOVATION is an act of subversion.

Just before Satoshi Nakamoto published his 2008 white paper on the rudiments of Bitcoin, it must have been a bit like holding a lit match over dry forest underbrush. Did he linger for a moment before hitting enter?

Maybe in that moment he closed his eyes and saw flashes from the future: of a thousand pimply geeks becoming millionaires overnight. Of Ross Ulbricht, Silk Road's Dread Pirate Roberts, being led away in handcuffs. Of mutant strains, copycats, forks, and tokens competing in an entire ecosystem of cryptocurrencies as in a digital coral reef. Of booms and busts and troughs of disillusionment.

We don't know. But we do know one thing about Satoshi Nakamoto: he hit enter.

A coder strings together lines of instruction. Once he publishes his code, there is a potential butterfly effect. Technological change, happening moment to moment around us, adds up quickly. Before you know it, people everywhere are taking rides with strangers. Bangladeshi women ply their produce trade on smartphones. Every wingbeat is a potential gale of creative destruction. A billion lines of code, created by millions of coders, represent innumerable wingbeats. Some are amusements. Others are bold experiments in social transformation.

Innovators' work reorients us by changing our incentives, which changes our behaviors. Or at least that's what I'll argue. And the work of *subversive innovators* changes the game. By the way, subversive innovation is not the same thing as disruptive innovation—though I doff my hat to Clayton Christensen. Where disruptive innovations in Christensen's sense "make products and services more accessible and affordable, thereby making them available to a much larger population,"[79] subversive innovations, whether or not they also qualify as disruptive in that sense, are those that have the potential to replace long-accepted mediating structures of society.

These structures are the hierarchies we trust and accept as a given. They are now vulnerable. Banks. Universities. Government itself. In other words, subversive innovation has the power to eliminate middlemen. When we consider all the mediating structures in the contemporary world, the implications are staggering. But let's not get ahead of ourselves.

The Singularity Is Somewhat Near

Here's a striking number: 97,900,000. That's how many results Google says the search term "artificial intelligence" returns as of this writing—and it will probably be higher by the time you read this. From chess-playing supercomputers to robot overlords, the idea of thinking machines has become something of a worldwide obsession. How long before we simply commune with AI in our heads as if consulting some benevolent oracle?

Among the 97,900,000 results, we'd surely find references to John von Neumann, the polymath and inventor. In 1950, von Neumann wrote: "The accelerating progress of technology and changes in the mode of human life give the appearance of approaching some essential singularity in the history of the race beyond which human affairs, as we know them, could not continue."[80] Maybe some sentient AI in the future will honor von Neumann as a kind of urcreator, along with Babbage, Turing, and Wiener, if such honors can be coded.

But what is a singularity? Or, more specifically, what is the *technological* singularity? In the 1960s, I. J. Good offered a clue:

> Let an ultraintelligent machine be defined as a machine that can far surpass all the intellectual activities of any man however clever. Since the design of machines is one of these intellectual activities, an ultraintelligent machine could design even better machines; there would then unquestionably be an "intelligence explosion," and the intelligence of man would be left far behind. Thus the first ultraintelligent machine is the *last* invention that man need ever make, provided that the machine is docile enough to tell us how to keep it under control.[81]

Science fiction author Vernor Vinge ran with Good's great idea. And in a now-famous 1993 essay,[82] Vinge describes a not-so-distant future in which machine superintelligence has brought the human age to an end. "Large computer networks (and their associated users) may 'wake up' as a superhumanly intelligent entity," Vinge writes.

What does it mean for machines to wake up, exactly?

Enter Ray Kurzweil. In *The Age of Spiritual Machines,* Kurzweil applies the logic of Moore's Law: roughly, that processing chips get twice as powerful every two years. Kurzweil invites us to imagine an era in which not only could our evolved brains be replaced for nearly any task by AI, but advances in related fields would yield sentient beings. These won't just be advanced computing devices. They'll be self-aware—in effect, animate instead of inanimate. Kurzweil thus popularized the idea of the singularity and gave his predictions evidentiary support.

Using the rationale of exponential innovation, Kurzweil forecast the point that AI superintelligence would emerge, almost down to the year. Kurzweil envisioned a time in which these "spiritual machines" would be able to solve a host of human problems, enabling us to live longer, and interface with us, perhaps within some networked All-mind. But not everyone was so optimistic as Kurzweil.

In 2000, having reviewed a draft of *The Age of Spiritual Machines*, computer scientist Bill Joy poured cold water on the enthusiasm, but not before conceding the basic premise.

"Each of these technologies also offers untold promise," Joy admitted in *Wired*. "The vision of near immortality that Kurzweil sees in his robot dreams drives us forward; genetic engineering may soon provide treatments, if not outright cures, for most diseases; and nanotechnology and nanomedicine can address yet more ills. Together they could significantly extend our average life span and improve the quality of our lives."[83]

Cures. Longer life spans. Improved quality of life. Millions of readers wanted in, but Joy was fearful.

"Yet, with each of these technologies, a sequence of small, individually sensible advances leads to an accumulation of great power and, concomitantly, great danger."[84]

It's the danger of unintended consequences. In complex systems, these can be compounded and replicated and become tough to reverse. Whether in CRISPR, genetic algorithms, or artificial intelligence, Joy was warning us about the unpredictability of nature, of which AI is but an extension. The Joy-Kurzweil debate created something like a permanent controversy.

Currently, titans like Elon Musk and Jeff Bezos trade barbs on social media. Musk has more or less taken up Joy's view. Bezos follows Kurzweil in his optimism. And as the titans argue, pundits join the fray. Perceptions on the prospects and perils of advanced AI have become a cottage industry: 97,900,000 and counting.

Yet in all of it, few deny that the singularity is coming. No one wants to be neutral in one of history's most important debates, but we'd be wise to consider both perspectives. Picking sides isn't my goal here, anyway.[85] I want instead to set the stage. As everyone looks to the horizon to scan for advancing robot armies, unemployed laborers, or both, a quieter revolution is unfolding around us.

Coevolution: Tools, Rules, and Culture

A line attributed to philosopher and social commentator Marshall McLuhan provides guidance. "We become what we behold," he reputedly said. "We shape our tools and then our tools shape us."[86] Whether McLuhan said it or not, it is on this single insight that our thesis turns.

Before we get into it, let's add a variation to the maxim: "We become what we *follow*. We shape our *rules*, and then our *rules* shape us."

Think about it: A decade ago, it would be virtually unheard of to get into a car with a stranger. It would also have been odd to stay in a stranger's bedroom. Today the hitchhiker taboo has been neutralized, more or less. The technology behind the sharing economy has normalized these behaviors, because the soft-ware injects security and reputation into what were once potentially dangerous activities.

Technology and culture thus coevolve. This vacillation occurs in waves as tech-nology changes culture, which changes technology, which changes culture, and so on through time. The advent of paper money gave rise to an economic revo-lution of global trade. Global trade gave rise to the advent of double-entry ac-counting. And modern accounting methods gave rise to the wealthy merchant classes of Italy, who sparked the Renaissance.

"He who wants to know how to keep a ledger and its journal in due order must pay strict attention to what I say,"[87] Luca Pacioli wrote of the Venetian system in 1494. Here, a system of profit and loss was made explicit and easily quantifi-able. One might argue that this innovation created a robust market culture. If you could measure activities that created customer value, you could do more of that activity. That's just good business.

During the Renaissance the optical lens came onto the scene, too, which chal-lenged the orthodoxies of world religions (think Galileo) and galvanized the sciences. Science, the enterprise of observation, needed more tools as it gob-bled up mindshare. Eventually the scientific worldview challenged religion as the dominant currency of belief. And as those tools proliferated, cultures began to change. Great swaths of humanity adopted new values. A commercial-scien-tific value system came to predominate in Europe and America. It spread like wildfire, giving rise to new innovations and cultural forms.

Fast-forward to 1960.

The FDA approved G. D. Searle & Company's Enovid, the first oral contraceptive. We know it as "the pill." Arguably, this event sparked—especially for women—the sexual revolution, which by 1968 was in full flower. Sexual norms changed, and women had far more control over both their sex lives and reproductive choices. Then, of course, with sexual independence came more career options and a wave of feminism.

Today, technology has broadened and deepened the sexual revolution—for better or worse. Apps like Tinder reduce the transaction costs of dating and mating. Japanese youth move online and away from each other, as hentai (explicit anime) hastens their demographic downward spiral. And young people everywhere are now freezing their sperm or eggs to delay parenthood—often to have more adventures before settling down. Tools. Culture. Tools.

Back and forth it goes.

But what about the rules? These invisible incentive systems Nobel laureate Douglass North called "institutions," coevolve with culture, too. Economic history supports the idea that institutions can shape cultural values. Following is North, from his Nobel Memorial Prize lecture:

> The organizations that come into existence will reflect the opportunities provided by the institutional matrix. That is, if the institutional framework rewards piracy then piratical organizations will come into existence; and if the institutional framework rewards productive activities then organizations—firms—will come into existence to engage in productive activities.[88]

Institutional economics, long ignored by the wizards of macroeconomics, supplies a quiet corrective to a discipline that has drifted into the obscurity of mathematical models. North's insight, that the rules provide a latticework of incentives powerful enough to shape our values, operates in the background here, too.

It's important to point out that the arrow of causation goes both ways. Thinkers like Deirdre McCloskey caution us not to reduce everything to a crude institutional behaviorism, but we must respect just how powerful the rules of the game are in shaping society. Still, if technology can transform culture and institutions, *catalyzing* social change becomes more than just a possibility.

For considering two vastly different sets of rules, the twentieth century offers us a couple of enormous A/B tests.

After World War II, the major powers carved up Germany. East Germany became communist and West Germany became capitalist. These two vastly different ways of organizing society, through two starkly different sets of institutions, offered us a natural experiment. By 1989 it was obvious that West Germany was far more prosperous and less authoritarian, and one could see the contrast simply by looking. On one side of the Berlin Wall, for example, lay bright commercial thoroughfares, while dreary brutalism lay on the other. But what had emerged in the hearts and minds of the two peoples over those years?

A group of behavioral economists wanted to study the differences between cultural values after years in different institutional settings. Specifically, the team of Lars Hornuf of the University of Munich, and Dan Ariely, Ximena Garcia-Rada, and Heather Mann of Duke University ran a test to determine Germans' willingness to lie for personal gain. Some 250 Berliners (the citizens, not the doughnuts) were randomly selected to take part in a game where they could win up to eight dollars. And the game involved opportunities to gain through lying and cheating.[89]

According to the *Economist*, after wrapping up the game, the players had to fill out a form that "asked their age and the part of Germany where they had lived in different decades." The researchers concluded that, on average, those participants with East German roots cheated twice as much as those who had grown up in West Germany. The team also looked at how much time the participants had spent in either place prior to the fall of the Berlin Wall. "The longer the participants had been exposed to socialism, the greater the likelihood that they would claim improbable numbers of high rolls."[90]

Why did these two groups perform so differently?

The study did not prove what caused the different behaviors. But we can speculate. First, we can safely rule out the hypothesis that East Germans were born with a predilection to cheat and lie. Both sets of Germans came from more or less the same genetic stock. It's also doubtful that the differences in moral outlook came from differences in, say, diet. The likeliest explanation for the difference is that the two vastly different sets of rules eventually shaped the values of the two peoples. *We become what we follow. We shape our rules, and then our rules shape us.*

Think about what you would have to do to get by in these two different societies. The late urbanist Jane Jacobs called these "systems of survival." The two different strategies, respectively, are taking and trading. That is, we can take what we need from others, or we can produce and exchange for what we need. Each of these strategies has a corresponding set of values, or "syndromes," which can be considered virtuous or vicious depending on one's perspective. According to Jacobs, takers tend to embrace "guardian syndrome." Among the prime values of guardian syndrome are loyalty, obedience, and knowing one's place. Traders, on the other hand, tend to follow "commerce syndrome." The values of commerce syndrome include industriousness, efficiency, and honesty.

Depending on circumstances, society can require both syndromes. But the values of guardian syndrome are the values that go along with shoring up hierarchies. The values of commerce syndrome are the values that coincide with creating networks of trade and collaboration. Crudely put, these are the values of the public and private sectors, respectively. And in the case of East and West Germany, we have two real-world analogues. Indeed, Jacobs lists one of the foremost values of guardian syndrome: "Deceive for the sake of the task."

Honor, Dignity, and Victimhood

Other compelling research appears to validate the idea that culture can emerge from institutions. Sociologists Bradley Campbell and Jason Manning[91] identify three primary cultural types: honor culture, dignity culture, and victim culture.

Within "honor culture," you might be challenged to a duel or a honky-tonk bar fight.

"Because of their belief in the value of personal bravery and capability, people socialized into a culture of honor will often shun reliance on law or any other authority even when it is available, refusing to lower their standing by depending on another to handle their affairs."[92]

In the American South, mediating legal structures such as law and courts were historically not so well developed as in the North. Honor culture was therefore more pervasive.

Within "dignity culture," one relies far more heavily on mediating legal structures.

"It is even commendable to have 'thick skin' that allows one to shrug off slights
and even serious insults," write Campbell and Manning. And "in a dignity-
based society parents might teach children some version of 'sticks and stones
may break my bones, but words will never hurt me'—an idea that would be
alien in a culture of honor." Dignity culture says we should avoid insulting others, too. In general, "an ethic of self-restraint prevails."[93]

But what if mediating institutions are perceived to apportion justice unfairly or
disproportionately?

Campbell and Manning describe a "culture of victimhood" as

> one characterized by concern with status and sensitivity to
> slight combined with a heavy reliance on third parties. Peo-
> ple are intolerant of insults, even if unintentional, and react
> by bringing them to the attention of authorities or to the
> public at large. Domination is the main form of deviance,
> and victimization a way of attracting sympathy, so rather
> than emphasize either their strength or inner worth, the ag-
> grieved emphasize their oppression and social marginaliza-
> tion.[94]

It's fascinating to consider the culture wars in light of these three descriptions,
but what's relevant here is how they show that institutions matter to the forma-
tion of cultural values.

Notice how these three cultures operate in relation to some institutional matrix,
namely the ability to rely on some sort of mediating structure—trusted third
parties or middlemen. In conditions where mediating structures are weak, we
get more honor culture. In conditions where mediating structures are well-de-
veloped, we get more dignity culture. In conditions where mediating structures
are developed, but are perceived to privilege those of high status and marginal-
ize those of low status, we get more victim culture.

Our tour of emergent cultural values flows into a single question: Is another set
of values waiting to be born? As I have suggested above, subversive innovation
is likely to bring creative destruction to many of the mediating structures we

take for granted. So a new culture is likely to materialize within a more peer-to-peer state of affairs. Because that new culture hasn't been formally identified yet, we can only speculate about what might arise. And I will, leaving it to academics to study. For now, though, it's enough to say we go about the world as evolved beings shaped by our rules, our culture, and our technology. These forces operate in a complex interplay, at times complementary, at times clashing.

Coming full circle, our thesis is that technology has the power to change the rules and the culture.

Human Nature: The Fourth Force

You might be thinking: Wait a minute. You can't just mention "genes" and move on. Glossing over human nature would be ignoring an elephant in the room.

And you'd be right. We humans are more or less the same creatures that roamed the paleolithic steppe some 15,000 years ago. Our human nature is a powerful force—one that both limits and affects the three environmental forces discussed above. The cultural values of guardian syndrome and commerce syndrome, for example, live within each of us as genetic propensities. In our evolutionary past we evolved to be both raiders and traders to survive. If we had not, we would have died before passing the genetic torch.

Evolutionary psychology, that bane of ideologues, has something to say about human values. "Under a loose meaning of the term 'hardwired,' all emotions are hardwired by evolution," evolutionary psychologist Max Krasnow told me in an interview. "We have the particular constellation of emotions we have because of our evolutionary history. Dung beetles go gaga for feces, but we generally have the opposite reaction."[95]

Evolution is the only way for any emotion to exist at all. Such a fact should be obvious to most, but it's often missed. Emotion's evolutionary origin doesn't mean our environments don't interact with our biology in fantastically complex ways. It means that when it comes to social change, human biology is a major factor.

One of the most prominent theoreticians in the related field of moral psychology is Jonathan Haidt, famous for his book *The Righteous Mind*. Haidt describes a cluster of roughly eight "moral matrices," which he likens to "taste re-ceptors" on the tongue. They are:

1. Care/Harm
2. Fairness/Cheating
3. Loyalty/Betrayal
4. Authority/Subversion
5. Sanctity/Degradation
6. Liberty/Oppression

And in later versions, Haidt splits Fairness/Cheating into two:

2. Fairness/cheating as "proportionality" of effort
2b. Fairness/cheating as "equality" of outcome

Some observers have suggested, justifiably, that we might add another:

8. Private/Common, i.e., how to deal with possessions and territory

In any case, Haidt's moral matrices are dispositions with which nearly everyone on earth is born to varying degrees, unless one suffers from a birth defect. So we are not just acculturated with such dispositions, we are "hardwired" for them to be expressed. Thus human nature is the fourth force behind social evo-lution. Combined they are culture, institutions, technology, and human nature.

That's a lot of forces at play. And when these forces churn, life can seem quite dizzying.

Subversive Innovation Comes in Waves

Indeed, the rate of change has been increasing since about 1800, and change continues to accelerate. It would be difficult to overstate the role of technology in this process. It is our Promethean fire. Subversive innovation is therefore a cluster concept that embraces all four forces but puts technology first. As philo-sophical economist Deirdre McCloskey tells us:

> We'll do better to call what was born in Europe in early modern times, enriching the world during the nineteenth and twentieth centuries beyond all expectations, by some word without the misleading connotations of "capitalism."

> "Progress" is too vague and too loaded politically. If you
> like neologisms you can call it "innovism." But the best of
> a weak field seems to be simply "innovation."[96]

Innovation it is, but with a twist.

Subversive innovation's first modern wave included the Internet and services
like Uber and Airbnb. Cryptocurrencies ascended in the second wave, and the
technology they're based on is becoming more flexible and robust. These technologies promise to *disintermediate* people. Thanks to a mix of cryptography
and distributed ledgers, countless "trustless" interactions are now possible. But
the first and second waves are but ripples. Bigger waves are coming.

Futurists Peter Diamandis and Steven Kotler refer to "exponential technologies" that tend to double in power—or processing speed, or market penetration
—every year, while their costs go down. Some leap forward by orders of mag-
nitude. But rapid adoption of exponential technologies cannot occur without
corresponding changes to people's everyday lives. And therein lies opportunity.

Exponential technology that obviates trusted third parties has the potential to
transform our institutions, our incentives, and our behaviors en masse. And
much of it happens without anyone's permission. Technology policy analyst
Adam Thierer makes the case:

> For innovation and growth to blossom, entrepreneurs need
> a clear green light from policymakers that signals a general
> acceptance of risk-taking, especially risk-taking that chal-
> lenges existing business models and traditional ways of do-
> ing things. We can think of this disposition as *permission-
> less innovation* and if there was one thing every
> policymaker could do to help advance long-term growth, it
> is to first commit themselves to advancing this ethic and
> making it the lodestar for all their future policy pronounce-
> ments and decisions.[97]

As sympathetic as we might be to the idea of permissionless innovation, it
would seem that Thierer is, well, asking for permission on behalf of innovators.

People like the pseudonymous Satoshi Nakamoto, creator of Bitcoin, are not
willing to ask for permission. A thousand coders code, a million users adopt,

and eventually whole populations wake up in very different circumstances. In this condition, politics becomes a lagging indicator. Policy wonks become chroniclers. And politicians, left and right, all become a peculiar type of conservative—standing athwart progress yelling, "Stop!"

But you can't stop evolution. It's everywhere. The philosopher Daniel C. Dennett calls evolution "Darwin's dangerous idea" and compares it to a "universal acid": "It eats through just about every traditional concept, and leaves in its wake a revolutionized worldview, with most of the old landmarks still recognizable, but transformed in fundamental ways."[98] Something similar can be said of subversive innovation. It eats through just about every traditional structure and leaves in its wake a revolutionized world, with most of the old rules still recognizable, but transformed in fundamental ways.

But how does subversive innovation work?

Remember that above we touched on just how powerful institutions are, which also means they're difficult to change. In other words, once the rules become well established, so do the incentives. Those who benefit from those rules will generally protect the status quo. Even the simplest laws, once passed, create special interests.

Political economist Mancur Olson described the phenomenon of special interests as "concentrated benefits, diffuse costs." Olson was referring to the power of special interests, even relatively small ones, seeking government favors or protection. The special-interest state, Olson thought, is hard to reform because general-interest voters have neither the incentive nor the knowledge required to fight the various ways in which favor-seekers court politicians. Special interests take advantage of tax codes, subsidies, and the regulatory regime. Olson's theory thus explains the existence of everything from mohair subsidies to taxi medallions. To understand the behavior of people in the political economy, we need only to ask, "Who benefits and who loses most from this law?"

Olson did not live to see the first modern wave of subversive innovations.

Could he have guessed that innovators would develop exponential technologies that would flip the logic of collective action on its head? For example, if you could create a technology a lot of people really wanted (like Uber in places like San Francisco, where taxis are expensive) or desperately needed (like Bitcoin in places like Argentina or Venezuela, where the government inflates the currency), the *benefits* would be dispersed and the costs of maintaining the status quo would become concentrated on officials.

Today we see old-guard cartels fighting against a massive hive of new contenders. And there are fights, to be sure. But there are also changes where none seemed possible before. Who ever thought taxi cartels would face competition, even obsolescence? Who ever thought at least some in Venezuela would have a way to escape their hyperinflated currencies and form commercial relationships in the cloud, above President Nicolás Maduro's goons?

Subversive innovators look for ways to exploit the weak joints or leverage points of the current system. In some ways they're innovators like any other. The key difference, though, is that they are willing to take their ambition and ingenuity into the headwinds of the status quo.

And they're just getting started.

Recall that our four forces of social evolution don't operate in isolation. That means we also have to work at building real culture and community around all the new ways innovators are changing industries and institutions. It's a different way of thinking from the old frame, preoccupied as that is with politics, policy, and punditry.

Nick Szabo works in a critical overlap of computer science, law, and currency. In 2007, he proposed a new form of law, one grounded in traditional ideas of property and contract, but without a predatory state to back it up. Instead, the system he called "Juristopia"[99] would rely on contract rights encoded in software.

Now think of cryptocurrencies. These include smart contracts, ownership, and hard-coded scarcity—hallmarks of Szabo's Juristopia. And yet "-topia" does not indicate some platonic ideal. The common law itself is a thousand-year-old, market-tested innovation. It is only perfect insofar as it rises organically from the interactions of real people through time. Szabo merely observed these patterns of emergence as a legal scholar. Then he put on his computer-science hat. The result, arguably, provided the contours of what would become the world's first cryptocurrency: Bitcoin.

Building a culture of subversive innovation means normalizing decentralization. This new ethos provides a kind of filter through which innovators begin to regard the world—they too will look for ways to think within, and produce within, the framework of subversive innovation. Indeed, as more and more innovators start to think this way, the proverbial genie escapes.

The Human Algorithm

But even Bitcoin, arguably the most world-changing innovation of the twenty-first century, was "forked" in 2017. Two camps were bitterly divided about the Bitcoin protocol. The sides engaged in bitter controversy, from great tracts of sustained argument to social-media smart-assery. It got scalding until one camp decided to pick up its toys and play elsewhere. That is, one camp took the code in one direction, forming Bitcoin Cash. The other camp took the code in another direction, retaining plans to improve Bitcoin another way. Each of these forks evolves or dies, as do competitors like Litecoin, Dash, and Monero.

Forking code is analogous to what might be the most important aspects of social evolution: *voice and exit*. Another of the giants on whose shoulders I stand is political economist Albert O. Hirschman, whose work *Exit, Voice, and Loyalty* offers something much more than a clever way of looking at consumer behavior.

Let's pause on just such an example from writer Lenore T. Ealy: "Reflecting on Hirschman's legacy, it seems ironic that I have been of late engaged in my own contest of exit, voice, and loyalty in regard to my preferred bourbon, Maker's Mark." No offense to the late Professor Hirschman, but Ealy's writing goes down smooth:

> Last year, inexplicably, the price for a 1.75 liter bottle of this particular distillation of Kentucky sunshine—though perhaps the corn may come from Iowa these days—increased by $5 per bottle. That's about 14 percent. Not understanding the price spike, and finding it inconveniently consistent across all local liquor stores, I decided to have a taste testing for my birthday. I wanted to look for a bourbon with a similar palate, but that sold at a lower price. A few (perhaps several) sips, shots, and glasses later, it seemed that nothing really came close. . . .

> Having at least begun to contemplate exit by exploring my
> options, I was not yet ready to jump ship: I stuck with loy-
> alty.[100]

In the market for consumer goods and services, alternatives tempt us from time
to time. But sometimes the change is bigger than voting with your wallet. We
might want to change something big. And if we're interested in engaging in
what McCloskey calls the "sweet talk" of a peaceful civil order, Hirschman's
human algorithm goes well beyond whiskey.

Getting down to brass tacks, there are only two means of social change—persuasion and coercion. Coercion means violence or the threat of violence. Because violence and threat are generally destructive, we want to avoid it where
possible. To change a system we're not happy with, we prefer persuasion.

Persuasion, then, involves two basic options: "Voice" is an act of speech and
expression within a system. It's an approach designed to convince others to accept change within a system, something like "I think we should do X instead of
Y"; "Exit" is an act of leaving the system to start something new. Of course,
when you start something new, you usually have to persuade others to join you.

If we are to avoid the threat of violence, voice and exit are the only avenues of
change. And yet, voice can be particularly ineffective in the face of both loyalty
and those who benefit directly from the status quo. So, when it comes to creating opportunities for exit, subversive innovators have to get creative.

In thinking of exit, we have evoked visions of whiskey and Bitcoin. But opportunities for exit are cropping up in strange and wonderful places. One of the
most compelling is in French Polynesia, a French "overseas collectivity" best
known for the island of Tahiti. But we're not just talking about leaving our boring corporate jobs to live on a tropical island. We're talking about a creative
way of building a new legal system on the ocean: seasteading.[101]

Imagine a cluster of floating platforms twelve miles off the Tahitian capital and
port city, Papeete. Upon these floating platforms an economic ecosystem forms,
with alternative legal frameworks operating on each. Research centers are
working on curing aging. Refugee innovators fleeing regulators on land are
launching startups. The cluster offers medical tourism, tax havens, and server
farms. If you can imagine this innovation, you're not alone.

In 2017, the president of French Polynesia, Edouard Fritch, signed a memorandum of understanding[102] that would allow private interests to bring both technical innovations (floating platforms) and legal innovations (seasteading law) to the Tahitian coast. If successful, these "aquapreneurs" might be the first to settle the blue frontier.

The core idea, though, is that seasteading creates as many opportunities for exit as it creates new jurisdictions. It is, following Robert Nozick, a "utopia of utopias," which is a clever way of saying that people can have different preferences about the kind of system they want to live under, limited by the system's ability to attract those exiting from other systems.

The Social Singularity

If social change is about creating opportunities for exit, it's not just computer coders who hold the Promethean fire. Subversive innovators look for weak joints and leverage points in any system. And if the opportunity is great enough, or the goal noble enough, they'll find a way. As each pursues various pathways, there will undoubtedly be pushback. Those who benefit from old ways of doing things will fiercely guard outdated systems. But gradually, the social singularity will arrive.

What is the social singularity exactly?

Recall McLuhan's thesis: "We shape our tools, and then our tools shape us." But how are we being shaped, exactly? Von Neumann's original formulation of the singularity is apt: "Some essential singularity in the history of the race beyond which human affairs, as we know them, could not continue." The social singularity will mark an end and a beginning. But the beginning of what?

The paradox of being human is that we are simultaneously competitive and collaborative, just like life in the natural world. Coral reefs, both cognitive and creative, are sprouting up everywhere. If this growing complexity could be measured meaningfully as information, such data would fry the neural circuitry of any single mind. Nobel economist Friedrich A. Hayek's insight is relevant here: knowledge is distributed among billions of minds.

How, beyond the price system, can we better coordinate those minds? How can we create new systems that unlock human potential, opportunities to work in synchrony for common missions, and idle capital? Not all human activity is governed by market prices. And market prices, though powerful, can be improved upon by better coordination technologies, better user interfaces, and ways to harness incentives to resolve collective action problems.

The structure and function of society emerges from our ability to reckon with complexity. We don't know exactly what these structures will look like in the future, but we do know that they will accommodate global flows of ideas, information, and creative relationships.

When this transition happens around the world, the social singularity will have arrived.

With matters sketched in this way, we should pause to think about four important indicators:

1. Mass adoption of secure networking technologies, which can enable us to cope with increased complexity, will cause a phase shift to occur.
2. As we enter the phase shift, certain mediating structures will become obsolete.
3. New forms of collective intelligence will emerge from networked minds rewarded by new systems of incentives.
4. We will collaborate as never before, and in ways that will be surprisingly well suited to our evolved brains and bodies.

Later, we'll go deeper into the nature of the phase shift that will bring about the social singularity. For now, though, we should turn to the nature of innovation itself.

The Race to Convergence

In *The Rational Optimist,* science writer Matt Ridley argues that today's technological abundance is a consequence of ideas having sex.[103] That is, human beings take recipes and recombine them with other recipes, which get tried in the world's innovation landscapes.

In *The Evolution of Everything,* Ridley takes matters further, by showing the compounding effects of innovation and change. In other words, it's not just that technological evolution happens, it's that it builds upon itself: "The explanation for the bizarre regularity of Moore's Law and its brethren seems to be that technology is driving its own progress,"[104] Ridley writes. "Each technology is necessary for the next technology."[105] Is it possible to extend Ridley's Moore's Law extrapolations to the domain of human collective intelligence?

Roughly, such forecasting can be formulated via a corollary to Metcalfe's Law, a law stating that "the value of a network is proportional to the square of the number of connected users of the system (n^2)." My corollary is that "the rate of progress in the emergence of collective intelligence is proportional to the rate at which we can organize ourselves into different kinds of human networks and develop superior knowledge processes." Thanks to disintermediation technologies, we're quickly self-organizing into these networks, which means we're sharing and recombining technological recipes at a faster rate.

Theoretical biologist Stuart Kauffman calls these kinds of recombinations "the adjacent possible." In the natural world, for example, the atomic constituents in the earth's primordial soup had first to form simple molecules, then more complex organic molecules, and so on. We couldn't go straight to cells or people, though. Each combination and recombination formed a new vector of biological possibility, which would present another vector in turn. Writer Steven B. Johnson describes the phenomenon beautifully:

"The strange and beautiful truth about the adjacent possible is that its boundaries grow as you explore them. Each new combination opens up the possibility of other new combinations."[106]

Johnson asks us to imagine a house that miraculously expands with each door you open.

"You begin in a room with four doors, each leading to a new room that you haven't visited yet. Once you open one of those doors and stroll into that room, three new doors appear, each leading to a brand-new room that you couldn't have reached from your original starting point. Keep opening new doors and eventually you'll have built a palace."[107]

Returning to technological innovation, we're opening doors into rooms of fractal palaces that could have been conceived in the mind of Escher or Borges.

Cycles of innovation that might have taken a hundred years have been cut to fifty, and then to twenty-five, and so on. How long can this halving of innovation cycles continue into the future? I cannot say. Indeed, some argue that innovation is slowing. But upgrades to our systems of collective intelligence mean that we are likely to get better and faster at sharing recipes, as well as at building upon and recombining them. In this way, you might think of the singularity and the social singularity as being parallel tracks. So it's not just that the machines are getting smarter. We're getting smarter, too.

In the meantime, it's as if we're all waiting around for AI to develop to a point beyond which it in some sense "wakes up." That would mean, at least, that technology becomes capable of being conscious, learning, replicating itself, evolving, and having an interest in its own continued existence. Such properties, though they are not all that makes us human, would be enough to make AI's attainment of them a historic flashpoint of enormous dimensions.

In the case of the social singularity, humanity, within some technological ecosystem, will evolve to a point beyond which the way we organize ourselves in relation to each other gets completely transformed. What that transformation looks like exactly remains to be seen. But we have clues. We can observe patterns. And we can speculate. The trendlines suggest we're getting better at collectively building on our knowledge base, as termites collectively build upon a mound.

It might be useful to think of the singularity and the social singularity as two separate processes racing forward in time: only one can win. Such might lead the pessimists among us to conclude the only way to ward off the negative effects of the technological singularity is to curb the advances of AI. But I'm not so sure. Maybe it's possible to network our minds to better harness our smarts. Even if we think of the two processes as a race, hopefully the social singularity arrives first so that together we can compete with AI, at least for a while.

But perhaps it's more useful to think of the singularity and the social singularity as two aspects of the same underlying process. Viewing matters this way, we might be led to imagine not two phenomena fundamentally at odds, but strands waiting to be woven together.

CHAPTER FOUR

REDISCOVERING OUR HUMANITY

An experience is not an amorphous construct; it is as real an offering as any service, good, or commodity.

— B. Joseph Pine II and James H. Gilmore[108]

IN 2016, Google AI's AlphaGo program won its third go match against Lee Sedol, one of the game's most dominant players. The ancient game of go has long been considered uncrackable in terms of AI programming. Not only did Google crack go, it was the first time a program had won so decisively. For many, it portended the end of human domination of planet Earth.

To hand-wring is human. If you've seen any of the predictions of robot apocalypse, you'll find at minimum that *Homo sapiens* still tells the scariest stories.

One popular theme is that the robots will take our jobs.

Not only are artificial intelligence and automation likely to displace people across a number of industries, they say, but the displaced will not be able to find new jobs. Technology has already started eating up roles currently occupied by the poorest among us, they warn, jobs like checkout clerk and fast-food-order taker.

One of the tidiest summaries of our collective hyperventilation about AI comes from writer James Surowiecki:

> Over the past few years, it has become conventional wis-
> dom that dramatic advances in robotics and artificial intelli-
> gence have put us on the path to a jobless future. We are
> living in the midst of a "second machine age," . . . in which
> routine work of all kinds—in manufacturing, sales, book-
> keeping, food prep—is being automated at a steady clip,
> and even complex analytical jobs will be superseded before
> long. A widely cited 2013 study by researchers at the Uni-
> versity of Oxford, for instance, found that nearly half of all
> jobs in the US were at risk of being fully automated over
> the next 20 years. The endgame, we're told, is inevitable:
> The robots are on the march, and human labor is in re-
> treat.[109]

So people who have come to depend on these jobs to support themselves and
their families will be cast into the streets, forming legions of the dispossessed.

The rationale is simple: Why hire a factory worker at twelve dollars per hour,
when you can install a robot for ten bucks per hour? Why bring on a janitor if
C3PO can do the job better, faster, and cheaper? Who needs an accountant
when an AI bot can manage the books as part of a software bundle? The answers to such questions add up to massive unemployment.

In the scariest of these scenarios, we're expected to accept certain assumptions.
These are not totally unreasonable assumptions, but there's room for pushback.
Indeed, the good news is no iron laws of economics lead one to project permanent displacement. It is only creative destruction, which Joseph Schumpeter described as the "process of industrial mutation that incessantly revolutionizes the
economic structure from within, incessantly destroying the old one, incessantly
creating a new one."

Unless a meteor hits Earth, we can count on that. Otherwise none of these dire
predictions is as inevitable as gravity. In fact, there are a lot of things we already know about economics that offer us a glimmer of hope.

Liberating Labor and Capital

Economic history since before the time of Ned Ludd is a story of people finding ways to liberate labor and capital. Something as basic as a broom spares
hours of work compared to sweeping with one's hands. The mechanization of

the plow has reduced a lot of back pain, not to mention time spent cleaning up mule manure. The microprocessor has done wonders for writers, who once used Wite-Out instead of delete keys. While we might be nostalgic about churned butter and wine grapes squashed underfoot, we can now go straight to eating and drinking and leave churning and smashing to machines.

Henry Hazlitt, in his famous book *Economics in One Lesson*, urges us not to take for granted the blessings of progress:

"The belief that machines cause unemployment, when held with any logical consistency, leads to preposterous conclusions" Hazlett avers. "Not only must we be causing unemployment with every technological improvement we make today, but primitive man must have started causing it with the first efforts he made to save himself from needless toil and sweat."[110]

That's great, but *Economics in One Lesson* was published in 1946. The fear is: It's different this time around. Hazlett could not have anticipated cognitive computers like IBM's Watson.

As I write, I wonder if my work is next. An AI consumes all the masters of non-fiction. Then literature. Then it tracks biological and other responses from readers as they read, mapping these responses against tropes, devices, and formulas until . . . For a moment I'm consumed by the fear that a sufficiently advanced AI could write these very words. But could it?

Rise of the Machines

The arc of history tells the story of ever-increasing returns on innovation. So far, it's a story of liberated labor moving into an ever-expanding, ever-diversifying economy. Corresponding to that labor liberation is the freeing of capital, too. If you have more time to work on productive things like writing books, you probably have more surpluses for other things, such as bets on new businesses.

But what if super-skilled computers learn to do everything better? That is, before we have had time to figure out something more creative. Not to put too fine a point on matters: Human performance is improving at a linear rate while computer performance is improving at an exponential rate. If we dumb humans can do the math, there will be a point in the near future when computer performance outstrips that of humans.

Yikes.

That's how things are different this time. This assessment isn't entirely wrong, either. Just as buggy drivers and buggy whip manufacturers lost their jobs to Henry Ford, many machinists at the Ford Motor Company have already lost their jobs to automation. It's a process that will continue and at the very least will create a great churn in the labor markets.

One problem with dire predictions, though, is the assumption that human performance improves at a linear rate. Science writer Steven Kotler states there are neurological mechanisms for increasing human performance that remain relatively untapped: "Surfing is a thousand-year-old sport. From 400 AD until 1996, the biggest wave anybody had ever surfed was 25 feet. Above that, everybody—scientists, surfers, physicists, and the rest—believed it was absolutely impossible. Today, surfers are pushing into waves that are a hundred feet tall."

But that's extreme sports. What about performance at work?

"How much work do you get done during an average day?" Kotler asks. "An average week? Now imagine being *five times* more productive. Not five percent more productive. But five hundred percent more productive—meaning you can now accomplish on Monday what it used to take you all week to do."

Management-consulting firm McKinsey discovered the preceding result in a study.[111]

The secret at the core of this phenomenon, says Kotler, is a conscious state known to researchers as "flow." Flow is a brain state discovered, studied, and named by positive psychologist Mihaly Csikszentmihalyi. In a flow state we are fully engaged. We lose our sense of time. We are focused and perform at levels far beyond what is possible in normal brain states. Although getting into flow isn't always easy, it's a natural tool for personal optimization.

We shouldn't pop champagne corks yet, though. Robots might very well be 5,000 percent more productive by the time we figure out how to better tap flow states. (And we'll still have to sleep at night.) Still, there is reason for optimism in the human-performance field.

AI worrywarts assume that the rate of AI improvement extends to nearly every dimension of life and society. *The New Scientist* reports "there is a 50 percent chance that machines will outperform humans in all tasks within 45 years, according to a survey of more than 350 artificial intelligence researchers."

But is this really true?

Some of this concern depends on the timeline, as there could be a big difference between twenty years and fifty. We can also admit that machines are indeed going to be better at doing a lot of things; otherwise we wouldn't bother trying to program them. But we should also consider that we are figuring out ways to improve ourselves, too. Therefore, must we accept the premise that there will be differential rates of improvement between robots and people in all cases?

It's in these differences that interesting things can happen, as we'll see. But before we get into the nitty-gritty of what the world might look like in the near future, let's think for a moment about two major, overlooked factors: life in a condition of radical abundance and what I call the human advantage.

Radical Abundance

When thinking about the future, we can reasonably expect abundance. Not just any abundance. But radical abundance thanks to exponential technologies and, of course, AI.

Envision a future in which a couple of guys show up to your plot of land and within thirty-six hours you have a new home. We're not talking about wheeling in a prefab home. We're talking about complete construction—from the ground up—using a 3-D printer the guys brought in on a truck. By using less labor and cheaper supplies than conventional construction, 3-D printing reduces the cost of a new house dramatically. All this technology might seem like sci-fi, but it exists. In 2017, a San Francisco startup printed a home in twenty-four hours. By the time you read this, whole neighborhoods could be printed.

Perhaps more disturbingly, envision a future in which many of the things people want are virtual and, therefore, nonscarce. Before we get to the all-too-human things we can rediscover about ourselves, we should think about life with augmented reality, perhaps even augmented consciousness. What if the next step from VR and AR is a technological interface with your brain via the brainstem:

You lie down in the sensory-deprivation room, close your eyes to connect with the interface point. In the past it would have seemed barbaric to interface with the brain. Today it's done noninvasively. You automatically connect to the biometric indicators so your vitals can be monitored. Your friend, Sara, in another state, has agreed to let you "ride" her experience, which she exports as a series of sensory inputs. She is going to hear a DJ with lots of light. In ten seconds, you'll go along for the ride. Nine. Eight. Seven . . .

Such thought experiments might be unsettling to some, but science fiction is often the first step to innovation.

To date, the trendlines for better, faster and cheaper continue in all major industries except education, health care, and transportation. I'll pass over why these industries are lagging. Suffice it to say, for now, that most of the things we enjoy—from smartphones to smart clothes—are cheaper and more readily available than ever before. We tend to forget that all this affordable plenty is made possible not despite, but *because of* automation. As this abundance shifts to being *radical abundance*, most of this plenty will be accessible to everyone.

While it's true the things that create abundance can have a displacing effect on labor and capital, labor and capital always seek somewhere to go. The question is, where do they go? Where will they go in the future?

Before we explore answers, let's consider a few trends that could have a profound effect on humanity's flourishing.

1. **New Energy:** Energy is the master resource. If innovators can relentlessly make energy cheaper and more abundant, that will have ripple effects through the global economy. Promising nuclear technology such as small modular reactors will help to reduce health risks because containment is more efficient and proliferation concerns are mitigated. Renewable energy innovations in solar collection and storage will enable greater energy self-sufficiency and decentralization at a lower price.

2. **Cryptocurrencies:** Money is meant to be a medium of exchange and a store of value. As centrally issued currencies tend to be inflationary, cryptocurrencies tend to be deflationary. None of us knows what life would be like in a deflationary economy. Such a state would encourage people to save rather than spend, which would go a long way toward liberating humanity from dependency on debt. And as the currency each person holds

increased in value, even people on the lower end of the socio-economic ladder would gain purchasing power.

3. **Tokenization:** Not only do tokens enable ordinary people to invest and share in profits, they enable shares to be traded like currencies. This radical democratization of investment means the inclusion of more people worldwide into systems of mutuality and prosperity. Apart from managing one's investments, such inclusion requires no labor. So more people will be rewarded because they *didn't* eat the seed corn. (Perhaps tokenization will facilitate significant mass ownership of industries dominated by AI.)

4. **Superabundance:** I first wrote "post-scarcity," but I erased it. That phrase evokes too much magical thinking, but I think superabundance is fair. This is the development that people fear, primarily because AI, automation, and self-replicating nanomachines will make all of our stuff for us. But goods, a large swath of the economy, will be really cheap and plentiful—and owned not by the few but by the many, thanks to tokenization. Manufacturing, like agriculture, will be a sector most of us will be happy to leave behind.

5. **Effective Giving:** In a condition of radical abundance, more people will have more resources to give. But giving, to be effective, must be thoughtfully considered. Too much giving can create unhealthy dependencies. Too little giving can create an anemic social sector and civil society. As we become more effective in our altruism, the kinds of projects and ventures that enhance the welfare of the many are likely to be assisted by "smart commitments" (a variation on smart contracts), as well as experimentation in organizational forms that benefit all. This includes experiments in mutual aid.

These five transformations are just a handful of the seismic changes we can foresee. They offer hints about where liberated capital is likely to migrate. Of course, sustainable patterns of specialization and trade will continue to lift humanity out of poverty. But other massive changes we cannot foresee will emerge from the array of adjacent possibilities created by ideas having sex. We cannot anticipate them all. So we should prepare ourselves for a condition of being constantly surprised, hopefully without losing our sense of wonder.

Before returning to the question of where labor will go, let's consider just what gives people advantages over AI (at least for a time).

Human Advantages

One of the great things about being human is that we feel. You might not think emotion is that important. And if you're Mr. Spock, feelings might seem like curious artifacts of a primitive past. But emotion is more important than just crushes and hot tempers. It's a critical aspect of a multidimensional system of experience we call consciousness. And the miracle of consciousness is not merely that we have evolved certain pain and pleasure reactions to our environments, which we can experience. It's that we are *conscious at all.*

Consciousness is what makes up our lives from the moment we awaken to the sensation of floating in theta waves just before sleep. It includes the redness of Washington apples, the smell of bacon at breakfast, and the giddy waves of your first crush. It also includes gut feelings about a place or a person, like that guy at work who just can't be trusted. Conscious properties are the *what it's like* properties of experience.

But what is consciousness? And why does it matter so much?

For many, the following might seem like a theoretical diversion. But consciousness—*what it is like*[112] to be a human—is critical to our success as a species and to our medium-term success relative to AI. So what I am about to write may annoy the most cocksure AI prognosticator:

AI programmers don't yet have a clue about what it would mean to create a conscious machine.

That's because nobody really understands the nature of consciousness. Despite the fact that though some philosophers have been relegated to teaching undergraduates about Plato's shadows on cave walls, philosophers of mind—such as Jaegwon Kim and David Chalmers—deserve a lot of credit for challenging us to think about just how far we have to go before building sentient AI, even if they aren't in agreement about the metaphysical determinants of consciousness.

Take a moment to look at the margin of this page. What you are experiencing is part of your subjectivity, that is, your consciousness. Does it have a certain texture as a physical page, or are you using an e-reader? Whiteness is a familiar concept. But the whiteness you are currently experiencing—call it Whiteness X —is a unique property of your consciousness. That is, it's a property of your experience, not of the page. It is also not a neural firing, although Whiteness X *depends upon* your neurons firing.

Let's forget about Whiteness X for a moment and attend to the sounds around you. Can you hear a fan? A refrigerator's hum? A child playing in the distance? When you do that, it can be difficult to keep reading. You have focused your attention on other aspects of experience, Whiteness X and Noise Y, instead of these words. These sensations, Whiteness X and Noise Y, are real. And indeed, they are real *to you* and not *to me*. The nature of these properties is mysterious, but understanding that nature is essential to creating machines that think and feel.

We know that there is a strong connection between conscious properties and the physical universe. In fact, what most philosophers of mind, brain scientists, and AI developers agree about is: consciousness is part of the fabric of the universe. Some think it is related to entropy.[113] It's not a mystical essence or a ghostly élan that animates the physical brain but is somehow separate from it. Consciousness is a feature of reality. But there is a massive explanatory gap between the features of consciousness—such as Whiteness X and Noise Y—on the one hand, and features of the brain and the environment—for example, light waves, sound waves, axons, dendrites, and neurotransmitters—on the other. To repeat, no one yet has a clue how to bridge this gap. No matter how sophisticated the "thinking" parts of AI get in the next few years, we are a long way from building a conscious machine, a machine for whom there is *something it is like*, a machine that can not only think but intuit, experience, and *feel*.

By the way, none of this is to argue that we can never *in principle* create conscious AI. Many philosophers and neuroscientists think that precisely because consciousness is a feature of the causal-physical world (that is, reality), it is possible for *conscious* AI to be designed, or for unconscious AI to create conscious AI, or for consciousness to emerge within complex AI systems. I realize the latter thought might be chilling to some.

In some sufficiently advanced neuroscience, we (or the machines we've invented) might discover just how consciousness gets instantiated and then use advanced technology to instantiate it. To create conscious AI, it seems reasonable to think we will have to replicate the causal-physical processes the human brain does with all its interconnected modules and subsystems rather faithfully. These systems work as a harmonious whole and give rise to our waking lives and lived experiences. If AI doesn't have waking lives and lived experiences, then it will always be a bloodless sort of intelligence. A fancy algorithm.

I should admit that there are many philosophers of mind and AI researchers who think *we* are just fancy algorithms and that consciousness, as such, doesn't exist at all. And arguing that is a whole research enterprise. We'll have to leave that debate for now. Let's just say I'm not ready to deny the technicolor aspects of our waking lives.

So I'm not quite so worried about robots as many, at least not yet. There are simply way too many things that humans will be able to do better and more authentically than AI because, thanks to evolution, we are complex, holistic beings. And we feel.

Consider an analogy: we have been assisted for decades now by computers that create special effects. CGI technology has gotten really good. But no matter how good it gets, when we watch, we have to suspend disbelief. We have this sense, after all, that it's just not quite *real* looking. In fact, the better CGI gets, the more attuned we are to why it doesn't quite look real. This is known among animators as the "uncanny valley."

For the foreseeable future, there will be uncanny valleys in all manner of AI endeavors, such as attempts at literature, art, and sex bots. This is not to say AI won't assist us, but AI that's as creative, sensitive to cultural context, and empathic as we are is not likely to arrive in the next decade.

Again, there's no reason AIs won't someday be complex, holistic beings. But currently, AI only does narrow sorts of thinking, though extremely well. Put another way: AI is similar to a small slice of the recently-evolved region of the brain called the neocortex. But there is so much to the rest of the brain than this slice, and therefore also to the mind. Social psychologist Jonathan Haidt points out that we make many evaluations and choices every day that are neither deliberately controlled nor, in most cases, experienced as "full-blown emotions." He calls these evaluations and choices "intuition." And in a famous metaphor, he shows how they relate to our deliberate reasoning:

> In *The Happiness Hypothesis*, I called these two kinds of cognition the rider (controlled processes, including "reasoning-why") and the elephant (automatic processes, including emotion, intuition, and all forms of "seeing-that"). I

chose the elephant rather than a horse because elephants are so much bigger—and smarter—than horses. Automatic processes run the human mind, just as they have been running animal minds for 500 million years, so they're very good at what they do, like software that has been improved through thousands of product cycles.[114]

Haidt's metaphor is not mere literary window dressing.

Screenwriter Lisa Cron reminds us that people and characters need emotions and intuitions, because these are at least half of what motivates us. Cron offers the story of "Elliot," familiar to cognitive scientists, who was the patient of a doctor named Antonio Damasio. Elliot had lost a small section of his prefrontal cortex during surgery on a benign brain tumor.

Prior to his illness, Elliot was in a high-powered corporate job and had a happy thriving family. But by the time he saw Damasio, Elliot's life was a mess. Bizarrely, he still tested in the 95th percentile of IQ. His memory was great. And he could throw out a dozen potential solutions to any problem. His trouble was, however, he couldn't make a decision, whether it was what tie to put on or how to prioritize his work. He simply couldn't cope with normal decisions of work and life.[115]

How had Elliot become so lost? Damasio figured out Elliot was no longer capable of experiencing emotion. Elliot was so detached, in fact, he approached everything and every situation as if it were neutral. Or, you might say *he* was neutral. Try to imagine not feeling anything when you hear your favorite music. You might be aware of the notes, registering as a kind of hollow stimulus. You might even recall that the music once moved you. But now you regard it and the rest of the world as a sort of dispassionate observer who cannot care.

Because of his injury, Elliot couldn't establish any sort of value hierarchy. He didn't know what mattered to him and what didn't, which meant he was devoid of motivation. Human beings—functional ones—are beings to whom things *matter*. Or as psychologist Daniel Gilbert puts it, "feelings don't just matter—they are what mattering means."[116]

Feelings make us care. Our inner lives are thus unique phenomena that in a sense define our humanness in contrast to AI. And this suggests that, given material abundance, we will be drawn to those aspects of life that require both elephant and rider. So we're not only poised to rediscover our humanity, we're poised to create new industries around that very humanity. Evolution has provided us not just with values, consciousness, emotion and intuition, but also philosophical, literary and aesthetic sensibilities. Being empathic creatures, we have evolved the ability to imagine what it's like to be in another's skin and *feel with* them. In this fact alone, new industries are waiting to be born.

The totality of these human properties makes for a truly well-rounded being. Far from being stripped of opportunities, we will create new ones, letting AI be great at games like go. In a condition of radical abundance, we will see the reemergence of cottage industries. We will see the emergence of new industries. And we will see existing industries become much more conscious of consumers' individual needs and offer highly differentiated and customized experiences. This development will proceed by building on levels of the adjacent possible as people go from seeking stuff all the way to seeking transformations. In all of this we will discover new types of experience, and we will rediscover our humanity in what Joe Pine and Jim Gilmore refer to as "the experience economy."

The Experience Economy

Because our lifespans are limited, people crave experiences. Indeed, most people, when they think about lying on their deathbeds, don't think about their net worth or all the stuff they hope to accumulate. They think about the memories they will have made. Moments and memories, for most of us, are more important than material things. We want to say, "Man, what a ride."

According to Pine and Gilmore, the experience economy is a "long-term structural shift in the very fabric of advanced economies."

> The growth of the industrial economy and the service economy came with the proliferation of offerings—goods and services that didn't exist before imaginative designers and marketers invented and developed them. That's also how the experience economy will grow: through the "gales of creative destruction," as the economist Joseph Schumpeter termed it—that is, business innovation, which threatens to render irrelevant those who relegate themselves to the diminishing world of goods and services.[117]

We are already, according to futurist James Wallman feeling "stuffocation," or a collective sense that material possessions are not enough. People are fleeing to the experience economy in droves, he says:

> It makes us happier, it fulfills our need for status more effectively, it creates a life of far greater meaning, and it solves stuffocation. With material goods, if you buy something that isn't very good—like a pair of shoes that squeak —there isn't much you can do about it. But when an experience goes wrong, it somehow gets better each time you retell the tale.[118]

So even as we enter the so-called "post-scarcity" era, we will be less impressed by stuff. Yes, there will be radical abundance in material goods. But there will be a plethora of opportunities in areas where scarcity remains—namely in the human-centric industries of the experience economy. In these industries our humanity will become more valued, and our humanity will become more pronounced.

Let's explore seven dimensions of the experience economy. These are surely not exhaustive, but they give us plenty of fodder to make the case that this new kind of economy is poised to emerge.

Dimension One: Uniqueness and Aesthetics

Value is subjective. Some of history's most influential thinkers, including Karl Marx and Adam Smith, got this wrong. Our preferences are different from one person to the next. And this is perhaps no truer than in the area of aesthetics.

Take a fine art, such as painting, or a craft, such as pottery. Each work is unique, and in some sense we value that uniqueness. We're often more compelled by artwork when the artist has a reputation, when we have a context for the piece, or when we know the backstory. We are willing to pay twenty dollars for the simulacrum of hand-blown glass, but we might add a zero or two if we know that an artist toiled with molten silicon and used his own breath to create the form. The same can be said for paintings, craft dolls, and metal sculptures. Stuff just isn't that interesting anymore. It's stuff plus experience.

Often these items are imperfect. In fact, relative to what a machine might produce, each piece could be uniquely flawed. According to Japanese lore, a young man named Sen no Rikyu sought to learn an elaborate ceremony called the "Way of Tea." Rikyu went to tea master Takeeno Joo, who tested the student by asking him to tend the garden. Rikyu cleaned up everything and raked the garden until it was immaculate. He scrutinized everything to be doubly sure. But before presenting his work to Takeeno Joo, Rikyu shook a cherry tree, which caused a few flowers to fall randomly—imperfectly—onto the ground.

According to the Japanese tradition of *wabi-sabi*, Rikyu understood the true nature of the aesthetic. There is beauty in imperfection. And there is something interesting about the fissures in wood, the crack in a bowl, or the randomness of a splatter.

Natural-living enthusiast Robyn Griggs Lawrence agrees:

> Wabi-sabi understands the tender, raw beauty of a gray December landscape and the aching elegance of an abandoned building or shed. It celebrates cracks and crevices and rot and all the other marks that time and weather and use leave behind. To discover wabi-sabi is to see the singular beauty in something that may first look decrepit and ugly.[119]

Of course, it's not impossible for an artificially intelligent artist to iterate endlessly on patterns of aesthetics that most people tend to like. And indeed, many fine-looking designs might come straight from AI, developed perhaps as amalgams of popular designs from the past. But for many things, human beings will not want the popular or the amalgamated. We will want the uniquely beautiful, interesting, or novel, or compelling art forms that are these because we have imbued them with our humanity. We will want a lot of things wabi-sabi, because they mirror our imperfection. Experience will surround our goods like narrative metadata.

Of course, AI can give us random petals strewn about the garden, or notched irregularities in our vases, but surely we will prize the idea that our artifacts' creators had intentions, passions, and histories that we might have shared had we walked in their shoes or drawn the breath they drew to blow the glass.

Wabi-sabi lives on "the long tail." That is, as we enjoy more material abundance in better, faster and cheaper stuff, there will be a whole class of artifacts and objects that are out near the end of the distribution curve. Former *Wired* editor Chris Anderson wrote of this distribution of desires in *Long Tail*:

> The theory of the Long Tail is that our culture and economy is increasingly shifting away from a focus on a relatively small number of "hits" (mainstream products and markets) at the head of the demand curve and toward a huge number of niches in the tail. As the costs of production and distribution fall, especially online, there is now less need to lump products and consumers into one-size-fits-all containers. In an era without the constraints of physical shelf space and other bottlenecks of distribution, narrowly-targeted goods and services can be as economically attractive as mainstream fare.[120]

The Long Tail is a theory of expanding economic niches, which AI will paradoxically help us to realize. In fact, the farther out we go on the long tail, the more likely we are to find goods and services that are unique and that we prize for their uniqueness.

It might seem counterintuitive that one should value something for its uniqueness. And yet we do, particularly along the aesthetic dimension. In 2017, for example, a van Gogh painting called *Laboureur dans un champ* sold for $111 million at auction at Christie's. The poster version probably sells for eleven dollars at gift shops. Even if some technological wizardry enabled us to recreate the van Gogh painting as an exact duplicate, people would want the real McCoy.

There is something valuable in the rarity of the painting itself, as well as the context in which it was created. In fact, *Laboureur dans un champ* was the first painting the artist was able to complete after recovering from an epileptic seizure.[121] Of course, most people still won't be able to afford a van Gogh. But as more people shift from jobs machines can do to jobs they can't, there will be more painters and more original paintings. And many of us will find that we *can* afford original artworks by lesser-known artists whose creations resonate with us—and that we'd rather buy those originals than posters of van Goghs.

Dimension Two: Attention and Time

One of the more immediate but underappreciated scarcities is time. In a highly complex economy, people will be guarding their time more, just as customers will be competing for it. And decentralization will increase that competition.

Can we imagine, for example, corporate digital intermediaries like Facebook and Google starting to dissolve? These companies are reaping billions of dollars to show users advertising, which we tolerate to enjoy the rest of the content they bring us. Can't we imagine consumers taking more of those formerly-captured profits directly in a decidedly more peer-to-peer era? Might people *get paid* to watch advertising or videos? Read emails or articles? There could very well be a set of future business models in which the masses earn extra money by auctioning off their time. This is a future of redistribution not through force but through organizational design.

We shouldn't forget the law of comparative advantage, either, which should continue to play itself out over populations with different talents and relative costs, as well as with AIs possessing different aptitudes. What sorts of jobs will people be able to do to save others time so that they can be more productive? It would seem that robots as smart as or smarter than humans will dominate the time-saving space, for example, carrying out mundane tasks. But sometimes we want to free up our time from complex tasks, and we want to be able to trust that that there is care, intention, and sensitivity to the exigencies of the work.

Organization and productivity are important. But often the time that makes life worth living is time liberated. We long to have richer, higher-quality experiences when we do have time—whether in our amusements or in our social interactions. And these, at least for the foreseeable future, require a human touch.

Dimension Three: Adventure and Exploration

Imagine a continuum between amusements and sacred experiences. On one end of that continuum you have a $100+ billion game industry. On the other end you'll find people making journeys into the Peruvian jungle to experiment with psychedelics. In between there are virtually unlimited forms of adventure, exploration and peak experience.

But it's not just that we're living experiences and curating memories. It's also that experience is how we define and display status these days. Social media has made it possible to share our experiences with others in real time. We want to give others a sense that we are important by virtue of the kind of life we're able to live. It used to be that you signaled your status by driving a Mercedes. Today more people signal their status by posting pictures of wooden longboats on a beach in Thailand. Soon they'll be waving to us from the moon.

Joseph Pine, coauthor of the influential *The Experience Economy*, cowrote a later book titled *Infinite Possibility*. In it, he and Kim C. Korn envision something called the "Multiverse," a heuristic device that enables entrepreneurs to carve up the dimensions available for providing people richer, higher-quality experiences aided by technology. In the normal universe, Pine and Korn say, we have time, space, and matter. But technology enables us to imagine these as on-off switches.

- **Reality** (time, space, matter): A walk in the woods with someone you love. Dinner with a friend.
- **Augmented Reality** (time, space, no matter): Using your smartphone to find objects (GPS maps) or to chase lovable virtual creatures that are overlaid on the real world. Be careful!
- **Alternate Reality** (no time, space, no matter): Using digital tools to explore some aspect of the real world—affected by real people—often through nonlinear, networked stories or quests.
- **Warped Reality** (no time, space, matter): Visiting a Renaissance festival, Colonial Williamsburg, or any other experience that suspends or plays with time.
- **Virtuality** (no time, no space, no matter): Playing a console game, exploring a virtual world, or immersing in any such experience—whether on-screen or using VR headsets.
- **Augmented Virtuality** (no time, no space, matter): Enhancing a virtual experience with a device that allows your body itself to augment an on-screen experience.
- **Physical Virtuality** (time, no space, matter): Designing some object virtually, and then using a 3-D printer to make it a real, physical thing.
- **Mirrored Virtuality** (time, no space, no matter): Experiencing mirrored aspects of reality in real time, such as the tracking of viruses like the flu—or traffic patterns.[122]

These infinite possibilities for adventure, though aided by AI, will require a human touch for a long time to come. Humans simply get humans. And human adventures will be on offer as long as people want to see the world—real, virtual, or something in between.

Dimension Four: Environment and Energy

"You need to disengage," says lifestyle writer Steve Bramucci. "At least for small snatches of time. For your sanity; for your health. You have to power down, close out, and turn off every single device you've got."[123] More and more people are heeding this advice—not only because we're addicted to our devices, but because we're remembering that we are beings that evolved in natural settings. And we need to reconnect with nature for our minds, bodies, and spirits.

Remember when you were a child and this was intuitive? What memories do you have? I remember the sound of tides and the scuttle of fiddler crabs roving beneath the docks along the Carolina intracoastal waterways. I remember the Blue Ridge Mountains rising up in the distance until we arrived among them to be greeted by moss-covered rocks, gurgling streams, and emerald rhododendrons. All of this is a form of nourishment.

Reconnecting with the earth might not seem like an enterprise, much less a scalable one, but it is. Bioremediators are cleaning up after the Industrial Revolution. Bioarchitects are mimicking nature as they help us live more directly with it. Artisanal farmers produce agriculture on the long tail. Conservationists are exploring and preserving everything from the earth's wetlands to the wild deserts. Ecotourism is already a multi-billion-dollar industry. As clean energy options are getting better, faster, and cheaper, we'll enjoy more energy abundance with fewer externalities.

Dimension Five: Community and Relationships

"A social instinct is implanted in all men by nature," wrote Aristotle in the *Politics*.[124] Though Aristotle never met Darwin, the latter might agree. We're social apes, which is to say we evolved to look out for each other. We have the capability even to put our own interests aside sometimes, especially when it's to help those we know.

Human beings also need community, but real community is not just *being around* other people. The invisible threads that bind us together usually start through mutual dependency.

According to historian David Beito, before the modern welfare state took over their functions, voluntary organizations known as fraternal societies took care of orphans, established homes for the elderly, ran hospitals, and provided other such services. In 1910, at least one in three American men was a lodge member.

These mutual-aid societies provided other community benefits that, though less quantifiable, were vital to the social order.

"Societies dedicated themselves to the advancement of mutualism, self-reliance, business training, thrift, leadership skills, self-government, self-control, and good moral character," writes Beito. "These values, which can fit under the rubric of social capital, reflected a kind of fraternal consensus that cut across such seemingly intractable divisions as race, sex, and income."[125]

Twentieth-century centralization nearly obliterated these fraternal networks. Still, we're likely to see a variation on them return in the future. Our needs are likely to change by degree and kind in a condition of abundance, but the great dirigisme of the central welfare state is likely to disappear as we approach the social singularity. That means mutual aid is likely to return—only we'll have technological support. Paradoxically, we'll be both more localized and more globalized. New communities will emerge both on the ground and in the cloud.

So while our higher-quality relationships might still be limited to around 150, following Robin Dunbar's anthropological constant, there will be opportunities for entrepreneurs who can facilitate, catalyze, and deepen human relationships. At work, those who can forge productive and meaningful organizational dynamics will be valuable. Social entrepreneurs will continue to build out the charity sector and civil society. And culture will still be an exportable byproduct of robust communities.

Dimension Six: Love and Care

Contemporary life has segregated us roughly by age groups. But our elders need us and our children need us.

And we need them.

We are learning that we can afford to do better than warehouse those who need care. In fact, in a condition of abundance, we will create more and more industries in which children and elders have more meaningful social interactions—some crossing age divides as well as false categories such as "retirement" and "school age."

Eldercare and childcare are, of course, growing industries, but they remain in many respects trapped in old ways of thinking. As people remain healthy and active into their golden years, they will want to undertake more than shuffle-board and early-bird specials. They'll want to work, play, and contribute to society meaningfully.

Similarly, developing children are developing not in real society at all, but removed from society in artificially planned environments. If we truly love them, we will learn to integrate them into more aspects of our lives, just as people did millennia ago.

And what about love and care between partners?

We might be frightened by trends like those in Japan in which young people are falling for AI instead of each other. This multi-million-dollar virtual romance industry is as much an outgrowth of Japan's hyper-conservative cultural mores on sex and marriage as it is of the power of software developers. But there "is even a slang term, 'moe,' for those who fall in love with fictional computer characters," writes Tracy McVeigh in the *Guardian*. "A whole subculture, including hotel rooms where a guest can take their console partner for a romantic break, has been springing up in Japan over the past six or seven years."[126]

Robot partners seem like frightening scenes from a dystopian future. But are these any more frightening than a hookup culture facilitated by apps? All of these trends are in the eye of the beholder, but I'm betting most will continue to long for the sustained, meaningful joy that comes with deep partnerships between two people.

And these sorts of partnerships can be supported by counselors and coaches who have unlocked secrets to lifelong love. The Beatles sang, "Can't Buy Me Love," but there are numerous ways to help others along their partnership paths. As we start to rediscover our humanity, it will be humans who help other humans reconnect. Those who can help others enrich their romantic lives or bonds of friendship will continue to be welcome intermediaries, exceptions, perhaps, to the disorienting dynamism of peer-to-peer life.

Dimension Seven: Purpose and Meaning

"I don't believe there is a consensus on that question," said Siri, when I asked the digital assistant about the meaning of life.

Siri's right. And there probably will never be.

Social thinker and startup consultant Bijoy Goswami thinks that meaning used to be something that was largely external and, sometimes, imposed on people. The idea of authoring one's own life was foreign to most generations; meaning was largely about one's place in one's society, family, and religious group. To have meaning was to be defined by one's societal function or familial role. And to some degree, such a concept of meaning still holds.

But after humanity began to understand the material world, recognize human rights, and build a vast commercial culture, Goswami thinks, people could afford to seek out something else. We needed to make our own meaning.

"How do *you* do *you*?" Goswami asks of his friends and colleagues. "How do you *be* yourself?"[127]

These questions do not yet get asked in every city, thinks Goswami. But as the world starts to decentralize, cities, communities, and individuals will start to develop more frameworks for making meaning. We will start to cluster and coalesce around different conceptions of the good life, and we'll start to exchange meaning-making frameworks. For some, helping people to create meaning will be a great way to make a living.

What are the contours of such a vocation?

The first step is often to help people develop a sense of purpose. In fact, in the experience economy it could be that one's purpose is to help others find purpose. Purpose could be a career path or a spiritual one. It could be that one develops artistic talent or pursues a calling. But ends drive means.

As people pursue their respective purposes, they'll want to be more fully optimized along any number of dimensions. Physical health, cognitive abilities, and psychological well-being will be part and parcel of improved performance.

But no one is the same as another. Optimization has its limits. Whether in our talents and abilities or in our very personality, understanding one's strengths and weakness originates in looking for patterns of behavior that help to make up who we are. People who are attuned to those patterns can assist others in being their best.

In achieving one's goals or arriving at discrete successes, it is important not to become complacent. Our work is never done, because in some contradictory respect, the point of the journey is the journey itself. When we undertake the process of becoming, we are striving for excellence. We are undertaking the work and allowing ourselves as beings to unfold, moment by moment, in what the ancient Greeks called *eudaimonia.*

Roughly translated, eudaimonia is happiness or welfare. A better way to describe it, perhaps, is living well and purposefully. And as we exit factories and fields, we will be looking for eudaimonia in both work and play.

It is no accident, then, that meaning and purpose are intimately connected. And questions about the meaning of life will be as elusive for AI as they are for humans. Meaning is a process of continuous sui generis creation. So for now, humans have an advantage. We know how to author our own lives. When we do, we are participating in acts of cocreation that originate in unique circumstances and particular conceptions of the good.

This will be even truer in the coming age of abundance.

Humanity Ascending

Let's close this chapter with one more shot of optimism, so we can stumble into the future a little less fretful.

Some worry we won't be able to keep up with AI long enough to become one with it. Others will not be comforted in the least by the thought of a merger between Humanity, Inc., and Robot, Inc. For this group, the very idea elicits a repugnance in which bioethicist Leon Kass thinks we should find wisdom. To them I'd say: remember that people were almost universally horrified by "test-tube babies" in 1978. Today in vitro fertilization is common practice.

The digital devices that occupy so many of our waking movements have already become like umbilical cords to some great, digital placenta. And the automata that will busy themselves with saving our labor will come closer and closer by shades, till they're our right hands. We'll scarcely notice it. And all the while we will be turning our attention away from the world's drudgery and towards the things that delight and fulfill us as humans—all because robots can lend a hand.

"We are as gods, so we might as well get good at it," the futurist Stewart Brand famously said. I think he's right. I'd add that we're never more godlike than when we're looking after ourselves. But our salvation will not come from a regulatory apparatus like that suggested by Elon Musk,[128] nor will it come from fear and Luddism. Our salvation will come in multiple factors that include co-evolution with the tools we shape, and that shape us, however advanced. And maybe it will come from the development of novel enterprises.

Above, I set out the idea that while robots will take many of our jobs, that process will bring about a condition of superabundance in certain sectors of the economy, making a lot of our wants and needs more affordable. Human labor, I suggest, will migrate into more deeply human spheres. We will then create whole new industries using the surpluses of the superabundance economy, so there will be well-paying jobs in serving each other in ways only humans can.

I suspect some readers remain skeptical of the idea that humanity will be able to maintain control over certain spheres of activity as AI develops. Even if we humans migrate into the experience economy, for example, will it be a growth sector capable of keeping enough people in jobs? And will these jobs really pay that well?

Despite considerable assistance from AI and collective intelligence (CI), which will make us far more productive, it's still exceedingly difficult to achieve economies of scale with certain kinds of services. The economist William Baumol identified what he termed the "cost disease," which is a rather nasty sounding name that applies to cost comparisons between rising worker productivity in certain sectors like gadget production (manufacturing), relative to others like healthy-people production (health care). As we'll see, one man's disease is another's treatment.

Here's what Baumol figured out, according to tech writer Timothy B. Lee:

> Rising worker productivity in other sectors of the economy, like manufacturing, was pushing up wages. An arts institution that insisted on paying musicians 1860s wages in a 1960s economy would find their musicians were constantly quitting to take other jobs. So arts institutions—at least those that could afford it—had to raise their wages in order to attract and retain the best musicians.[129]

The result is that rising productivity in, say, manufacturing inflates the cost of labor-intensive work like musical performances. Rising productivity means factories can cut prices and raise wages, but when wages go up, concert venues have no choice but to raise ticket prices to cover their own higher labor costs. The question before us, then, is: Can we extend this rationale beyond factories and orchestras to all manner of goods and services, including those in the burgeoning experience economy?

Of course, we can imagine robots replacing people in all sorts of roles, including first violin of the New York Philharmonic. But just because we can doesn't mean they will. The so-called "prosperity paradox" works within industries, just as well as it works across them. And that means people are still willing to pay $4.50 for a cup of coffee served by a punk-rock barista in a unique setting, even though they could get a cup for $1.85 at Starbucks thanks to corporate best practices and economies of scale. You might call this willingness to pay more the "experience premium." And if you work in an industry with low productivity growth, you might also call it "Baumol's pay raise."

My hopeful prediction—in the medium term—is that we will see the emergence of countless new jobs of relatively low productivity growth, especially when compared with the superabundance sectors. Indeed, as we continue to architect the scaffolding of the much-maligned "gig economy," there will be a slew of opportunities to match buyers and sellers of unique services, just as Uber matches passengers and riders.

That we can create machines that are smarter and faster than we are on many dimensions is a testament to our human capabilities. And we're still smart enough to know where we really want our kin—those with whom we have specially evolved bonds. Still, we should not see ourselves as being at odds with AI, but rather see AI more and more as being extensions of ourselves. For in time, the line between man and machine might not be as bright.

CHAPTER FIVE

THE SOCIAL CONSTRUCTION
OF OUR NEW REALITY

In Esmeralda, city of water, a
network of canals and a network
of streets span and intersect each
other. To go from one place to
another you have always the
choice between land and boat:
and since the shortest distance
between two points in Esmeralda
is not a straight line but a zigzag
that ramifies in tortuous optional
routes, the ways that open to each
passerby are never two, but many,
and they increase further for those
who alternate a stretch by boat
with one on dry land.
— Italo Calvino[130]

MOST OF US WALK AROUND on planet Earth with certain programming. Biases. Tendencies. Preferences. Cultural baggage. In your first experience at Black Rock City, you at the very least become acutely aware of it. For a few days you can suspend the programming to some degree, maybe even leave some behind. Some of us need a bit of *deprogramming*—a few of us desperately. It invites us, after all, to acknowledge all the counterproductive memories, mores, or mental monsters, and ask what can be left out there to burn.

A great temple there invites you to come in and pray or reflect or meditate. When you do, pictures of people have been tacked up as makeshift shrines all around. Look up and a fractal of wooden beams climbs into the sky. Though it is breathtaking, in another day or so the temple will burn. Something else equally compelling will take its place next year. And it too will burn.

Buddha smiles.

Walk over to a tree of life pulsing with energy. It's an illusion created by projection mapping. People are sitting nearby in bonds of love, and the tree's energy seems to flow through them. You might scoff at illusions. But you can feel that energy all around you, even though it's started with eye tricks and music. Isn't everything in our mind an illusion of some kind?

What I have been describing is Burning Man.

I can't say what it is for everyone. I can say what it did for me. It reconciled contradictions: It is playful and hard. Sacred and profane. Left brain and right. Light and shadow. Wakefulness and slumber. The anima and the animus. The ecstatic and the reflective. It is love and it is death. And it fundamentally changes you, all while you are just discovering your constants.

There are no words, no videos, no pictures nor articles adequate to limn the experience. Yours is but one perspective among many thousands of perspectives, which still manage to be blind men's hands on a great elephant. Burning Man is a landscape of the ineffable animated by a city of lost souls. That's because we're all lost to some degree, so when you go you've found home for a time. Next year it will be there, and it will not be there.

Much of reality is socially constructed. Black Rock City—including its laws, its culture, and its aesthetic—is socially constructed. What has evolved there in the desert is far more than a kaleidoscopic coral reef of music and lights. It is a spiritual oasis that hovers at the intersection of reality and dream.

Invisible Cities

But what is "Black Rock City"? During certain parts of the year there's really nothing and no one there. The desert becomes an empty canvas upon which 70,000 artists will paint a new experience. When we think of a city, though, we usually think of something more permanent. New York City, for example, includes the Empire State Building and the Chrysler Building. And yet prior to the construction of any skyscrapers, New York was there, just as New York continued to be there after the old World Trade Center fell on September 11, 2001.

Neither Black Rock City nor New York City is the sum of its structures. These cities are also collections of people who come and go—clusters of laws, cultures and ways of life—places, proximate and approximate, situated on the earth. They're all of these aspects in a mix of physical and social construction. Buildings, people, rules, and ways of life constitute layers of reality. The invisible filaments of community bind all these layers together in novel ways.

Emergence

In every city, whether at Burning Man or within the Five Boroughs, there is emergence. Some call it emergent complexity, which is a mouthful. The best way to describe the phenomenon is complex, unplanned order.

"Cities have no central planning commissions that solve the problem of purchasing and distributing supplies," wrote John Holland, the late complexity theorist.

> How do these cities avoid devastating swings between shortage and glut, year after year, decade after decade? The mystery deepens when we observe the kaleidoscopic nature of large cities. Buyers, sellers, administrations, streets, bridges, and buildings are always changing, so that a city's coherence is somehow imposed on a perpetual flux of people and structures. Like the standing wave in front of a rock in a fast-moving stream, a city is a pattern in time.[131]

Frédéric Bastiat, the great nineteenth-century economic journalist, put Holland's question more succinctly: "How does Paris get fed?"

It's not just cities, of course. Emergent systems include language, coral reefs, galaxies, and rain forests. What all of these have in common is that they come into existence as if by an invisible hand. That invisible hand always includes some set of rules underlying all the complexity. For galaxies, those rules are physical laws. For the Internet, those rules are computer code. For cities, those rules are laws.

When it comes to emergence we have to be careful about the difference between rules and plans. The former enable order to emerge. The latter limit emergence.

"There is a quality even meaner than outright ugliness or disorder," wrote the great urbanist Jane Jacobs, "and this meaner quality is the dishonest mask of pretended order, achieved by ignoring or suppressing the real order that is struggling to exist and to be served."[132]

When Jane Jacobs wrote the preceding words in her timeless *The Life and Death of Great American Cities*, she was making an impassioned plea to the people against the planners of New York. These planners had decided that the organically grown qualities of the city—where neighbors made creative collisions on imperfect streets—weren't good enough.

Instead the planners would impose their visions by tearing down old neighborhoods and dividing them with highways. They'd move the poor into public housing and hope the jazz followed. The planners thought they knew better than the people. But Jacobs saw things differently. She saw patterns of interaction in the noisy and chockablock neighborhoods. She saw emergence.

Why was Jane Jacobs so intent on protecting those patterns of interaction?

Reality by Agreement

So much of life's bounty is invisible. That is to say it's both socially constructed and intersubjective. Intersubjectivity is sort of like objectivity, only without the pretense that we can ever step out of our own skins to verify what reality *really is.* Our relationship to reality is mediated by our experience. But I'll not belabor any philosophical questions. The point here is practical: much of the world works because people made *something* up and we agree it's real. Some would even say morality works this way. But let's take a simpler example: money.

Money is in many ways a collective illusion. What makes it so easy to believe in is its utility. When you give it to people, they bring you cappuccinos or cars. I'm oversimplifying things a bit. We know, for example, that if there is too much money floating around out there, it could take a wheelbarrow load just to get a cup of coffee. Still, money is a kind of useful agreement—an unspoken social contract. Even if we used gold coins as money, there is nothing intrinsic about the value of gold. (A massive gold meteor shower would disabuse us of that notion.) The only thing objective about money is its price, of course, but that is contingent upon the intersubjective agreement of valuers. Otherwise, people use it as a medium of exchange and a unit of account. As long as the monetary unit is relatively stable over time, money serves both functions. But the value of money is neither an iron law nor an objective fact.

As I suggested elsewhere, cryptocurrencies like Bitcoin have the potential to upgrade money forever. Coders can program the technical properties of these new forms of money, but a digital currency is still only as valuable as it is useful, and only as valuable as others in the network agree. Use value—utility—is in the eyes of beholders. Cryptocurrencies, like fiat monies, count on intersubjective agreement to be sustainable in the long term. And if cryptocurrencies continue to improve, as I've suggested, they could eventually outcompete currencies minted or printed by nation-states and central banks. The prices of cryptocurrencies can reflect irrational exuberance, to be sure. But they can also reflect the social construction of new, invisible realities, leaving old realities like "dollars" and "renminbi" to wither.

Journalist Maria Bustillos reminds us that all value is contingent upon the perspective of the subject. She writes:

> Our shared understanding of the value of that green-tinted piece of paper, that Krugerrand, ether token, or pound coin, is all that counts. And that shared understanding has no fixed meaning; it's in eternal flux. The "value" of all money, all stores of exchange, is unstable and abstract, even in the face of every attempt to secure it—say, with a set rate of exchange against various assets—or to regulate its flow by setting interest rates. Money is only a shifting network of agreements made in and on behalf of the hive, and that's all it has ever been—a fragile thread in a web of human trust.[133]

Now, one would not want to overstate things.

Dollars have network effects. Cryptocurrencies have network effects. Neither are mere mass hallucinations, but they are perhaps convenient fictions. Socially constructed realities like money and cryptocurrencies are made more real by their utility. So money is different from, say, social habit or convention. Technology has helped us to upgrade what was always a social construct. So the questions arise: What else can we upgrade? What else can we construct? And which social constructs have outlived their usefulness?

Coding Common Law

Many observers think Nick Szabo is the pseudonymous Satoshi Nakamoto, creator of Bitcoin. Szabo, you see, is the coding wizard and law professor we met earlier. He had already offered a proposal for digital currency called "bit gold."[134] And, indeed, in the late nineties, Szabo had already formulated the concept of smart contracts, a computer function that can facilitate transactions in the absence of third parties.

Szabo has written extensively on the history of law and money. In particular, Anglo-Saxon emergent law eventually collided with the "master-servant" law of Justinian's Rome. Szabo argues that what we have today in the United States is but a shrinking vestige of common law operating within a growing body of Roman-style statutes.

All this might sound esoteric, but it has profound implications for cryptocurrencies, smart contracts, digital property titles, dispute resolution, and other potential applications of the technology that lies at the heart of Bitcoin.

In 2006, Szabo wrote, "A franchise, such as a corporation, a jurisdiction, or a right to collect certain tolls or taxes, was a kind of property: an 'incorporeal hereditament.' English property law was very flexible; as a result, franchise jurisdictions came in a wide variety of forms."[135] But little remains. We can see vestiges of franchise jurisdictions in, say, homeowners associations. Some of these aspects of the common law are still with us, but most were supplanted by statutes. The flexibility and diversity of property in private law was crowded out.

So what happened?

> The Anglo-Norman legal idea of jurisdiction as property and peer-to-peer government clashed with ideas derived from the Roman Empire via the text of Justinian's legal code and its elaboration in European universities, of sovereignty and totalitarian rule via a master-servant or delegation hierarchy. By the 20th century, the Roman idea of

hierarchical jurisdiction had largely won, especially in political science where government is often defined on neo-
Roman terms as "sovereign" and "a monopoly of force."[136]

This militaristic law is so ingrained in our understanding now that it's difficult
for most of us to imagine life outside of it. (We make our rules and our rules
make us.) Our picture is of wise stewards minding the upper echelons of statecraft, while the rest of us teem and hustle in relatively peaceful interstices that
the regulatory state provides. It's hard to conceive of alternative forms of governance and law doing better. Peace is a product of Leviathan.

Most of us have been thoroughly inculcated with this Hobbesian rationale.
Consciously or not, most assume that any persistent peace requires a final ar-
biter—one whose might quashes conflict and whose law is made absolute
through enforcement. And when it comes to alternatives, our failure of imagination has given rise to some of the most predatory regimes in history. As Szabo writes:

> Our experience with totalitarianism of the 19th and 20th
> centuries, inspired and enabled by the Roman-derived pro-
> cedural law and accompanying political structure (and in-
> cluding Napoleon, the Csars, the Kaisers, Communist
> despots, the Fascists, and the National Socialists), as well
> as the rise of vast and often oppressive bureaucracies in the
> "democratic" countries, should cause us to reconsider our
> commitment to government via master-servant (in modern
> terms, employer-employee) hierarchy, which is much better
> suited to military organization than to legal organization.[137]

Indeed, we should reconsider our unreflective commitments to such hierarchies, because law and society are not only possible without them but could be
more robust, peaceful, and prosperous without them.

But how do we move beyond those hierarchies?

One can see how Szabo might appreciate the flexibility of the common law as a
software developer. For in that interest lies the notion that one could literally
encode law with computers and have others update it as necessary, as humanity's original open-source code. Whoever designed the basic protocols behind

Bitcoin understood the power of "dumb networks" as opposed to Byzantine command-and-control codes. Szabo writes:

> Fortunately, franchise jurisdiction has left permanent influences on modern governments, including on the republican form of government in general and the United States Constitution, federalism, and procedural rights in particular. It also left a record of a wide variety of forms of law and government that can provide us with alternatives to the vast employee hierarchies wielding coercive powers that have given rise to modern oppression.[138]

One of the basic questions of "good" law is whether people actually follow it. The inventor(s) of Bitcoin must have known that and helped us to imagine a different sort of code that weaves together legal code and computer code. And, of course, people are using it—all without anyone's permission.

Venture fund manager Michael P. Gibson leaves us with a bright glimpse of the future, a future in which we choose our governance. He calls it the "Nakamoto Consensus":

> It turns out there's only one thing that guarantees production of good laws. The people bound by the laws have to agree to be bound by them. Not hypothetically or tacitly, as in some imaginary will of the people or behind a veil of ignorance. Consent must be real, transparent, and continuous. No law can bind a single person unless that person consents to be bound by that law. All laws must be strictly opt in. Lawmakers could be saints, devils or monkeys on typewriters—doesn't matter. The opt out-opt in system lets only good laws survive. Bad laws are driven out of production.
>
> Bad laws can only inflict harm and destroy wealth up to the cost to opt out of them. We can underthrow the state one contract at a time.[139]

This insight—articulated so well by Gibson—is what surely informed Nick Szabo and inspired Satoshi Nakamoto.

Szabo is, in fact, a software developer who set about writing source code for peer-to-peer law. He wanted, in a sense, to "hard code" the common law. So if the "underthrow" of Leviathan lies ahead, it will be thanks not only to encryption technology but also to understanding the beauty, flexibility, and robustness of emergent law. Smaller jurisdictions created by forking the code or by allowing people to vote with their boats will be enough to reduce the costs of exit for millions looking for a better life.

Whether Nick Szabo is Satoshi Nakamoto, I cannot say. But at the very least, Szabo was part of a community from which Nakamoto drew knowledge and inspiration. And that community was built on ideas—both time-tested and new—that are being given expression in ones and zeros.

Programmable Incentives

"One of the first rules of economics is that humans respond to incentives," software developer Justin Goro reminds us. "Up until now, very few people have had the power to craft society-wide incentives without resorting to coercive force." But coders have a saying, which has both positive and normative connotations: "Code is law."

The importance of the insight that code is law cannot be overstated. In a certain sense, the social singularity will be built on it. Before we explore the implications, let's break down the ideas a little more.

First, the distributed ledger.

The famous blockchain on which Bitcoin is built is just the first iteration of distributed-ledger technology. And according to researchers at the RMIT University Blockchain Innovation Hub, Bitcoin is not likely to be the most important use of distributed ledgers.

"It might seem strange that a ledger—a dull and practical document associated mainly with accounting—would be described as a revolutionary technology. But the blockchain matters because ledgers matter."[140] Ledgers matter because they're a way to record facts. Distributed ledgers are digital systems that allow the simultaneous recording, replication, and global sharing of factual records. They use cryptography to ensure that everyone can have a reliable copy of the same database, but no one can alter it except according to the rules built into the software. That makes the records—in Bitcoin's case, records of financial transactions—community observable and tamper resistant. In this way, distributed ledgers will be as important to twenty-first century social organization as double-entry accounting was to the development of business.

But merely recording facts is not enough. It's also what can now be recorded.

Enter smart contracts. Smart contracts help people to exchange money, property, or anything of value in a transparent way—all while eliminating middlemen.

"The best way to describe smart contracts is to compare the technology to a vending machine," says Ethereum founder Vitalik Buterin. "Ordinarily, you would go to a lawyer or a notary, pay them, and wait while you get the document. With smart contracts, you simply drop a bitcoin into the vending machine (i.e. ledger), and your escrow, driver's license, or whatever drops into your account."[141]

With smart contracts and distributed ledgers, it's possible to create programmable incentives. That means economics is no longer about obscure models or retrospective explanations, but engineered, testable ecosystems of value created within peer networks. In short, says software developer Rob Knight, "what people mean by 'the blockchain' is just 'economics, on computers.'"[142] People can align interests in mass-coordination efforts voluntarily.

People, always fallible and sometimes venal, have long had to be the glue of other people. But along many dimensions those arrangements will pass away. Smart contracts, like those conceived of by Szabo and improved by brilliant innovators such as Buterin, allow us to remove fallible human beings from the equation—at least in a number of important circumstances. And in those circumstances, all manner of decentralized applications are made possible.

Developer Justin Goro thinks decentralized applications amount to being "a host of humans acting together to achieve a group goal." Instead of goodwill or trust, "the coordinating mechanism is the glue of blockchain secured tokens."[143] To fully grasp the implications, we have to consider how tokenization could eliminate certain kinds of middlemen and yet bind people together in the service of common ends.

The Implications

In the past, humans had to get big things done through different structures of social coherence. Whether it was allegiance to Queen and Country or fear of IRS agents breaking down your door, social coherence was achievable. But more and more, getting big things done will be carried out through biomimicry. That is, we'll act more like bees. Distributed ledgers aren't AI supercomputers like IBM's Watson that figure everything out or tell us what to do. In many ways, distributed ledgers are more like what Bitcoin expert Andreas Antonopoulos calls "dumb networks," only with pretty smart beings as nodes in those networks.

"They will act as the connective tissue between humans and machines, mediated by incentives," writes Goro. "If humans are neurons in the great human hive mind, blockchain technology acts as the connective tissue and neurotransmitters."[144]

Or, you might say, we'll create pheromone trails for each other.

When all the incentives are aligned such that people are being organized into hive minds, the game has changed. No power center is safe. Whether we're talking about big corporations or big governments, distributed ledgers are threatening to dissolve society's most powerful mediating structures. Such a claim might seem fantastic in the age of such awesome central powers. But consider this: what's powerful about decentralization is that it is carried out through the power of persuasion (instead of coercion). When you can incent millions of people all at once to change their patterns of behavior—and reward them for doing so—incentives align. It's in this mass alignment of incentives that big things get done.

Tokenization

Big things like what?

Take the example of an Uber-style tech company, offered by Brendan Blumer, Dan Larimer, and Brock Pierce.[145] With the traditional centralized tech firm, you have three different stakeholder groups, each of which is somewhat at odds with, or at least engaged in a kind of pulling against, the others. You have users (drivers), who are focused on extracting daily payments. You have users (riders) who want to get from point A to point B. And you have shareholders interested in seeing profits in the next quarterly report. There is no vested interest on the part of users. In this set up, the beneficiaries and the users have somewhat misaligned. The profit motive connects everyone to some degree, but that's the only connection. Users don't really care about the success of the company.

By contrast, distributed autonomous organizations create a different sort of incentive ecosystem—one in which users have more vested interest in the health of the company—by degrees. This creates far greater alignment among stakeholder groups. First, you have the token, which connects users, both value creators (like drivers) and value extractors (like riders), aligning the interests of everyone involved, including investors who can buy access to the DAO network. The currency becomes part of the product design or service offered. Because governance is distributed among token holders in a DAO, the enterprise forms a community based on the growing value ecosystem. Everyone can contribute. The DAO environment, in contrast to most legacy companies, is more transparent, accountable and trustworthy by nature. Everyone knows the rules, so greater predictability follows. The incentive alignment that comes about in the absence of central authority amounts to decentralized decision-making, as well as real options for detractors with a different vision. Token holders have skin in the game.

Imagine a tokenized version of Uber called Tuber. There is a token called Tubies, which you can easily buy and sell on a popular exchange. Drivers and riders use Tuber networking technology to connect with each other, just as they do with Uber. And just as with Uber, Tuber has standards and a fee request mechanism when, say, a passenger vomits on the back seat. In the case of Uber, this fee request was created and refined by a decisionmaker at Uber, perhaps after the company received angry driver feedback. But the code for the fee request system is proprietary and closed. The pool of innovation is thus quite limited. With Tuber, anyone, including an army of drivers and riders, has the ability to look at current standards, practices, and lines of code, as well as to suggest changes. That expands the pool of innovators. Remember, Tuber drivers are paid in Tubies, a native currency, every rider receives that token, and they, in turn, sell it back to people who need rides. So every single person in that corporate ecosystem now has a greater incentive to care about the success of the company—including its standards and functionality. It's as if drivers were getting paid with stock in Tuber. After all, their Tubies will *increase in value* if they suggest a valuable change. Now, because Tuber technology is also fully decentralized and open source — and doesn't even live on a server — it can't be taken down, nobody can seize control of it, and it is accessible by everyone. An army of programmers, paid in Tubies, is waiting for feedback from drivers and riders so they can be rewarded for upgrades and see the value of their Tubies increase. Likewise, there are people who satisfy all manner of roles within Tuber, having self-organized, who also get paid in Tubies. (Holacracy is one example of a process for corporate self-organization.)

Tokenization allows an enterprise—in part or whole—to embrace change because the enterprise has become a community and the community has become the enterprise. As Trent McConaghy describes it, the process "melts" into community with time. If some faction within the community doesn't like what's going on, it can exit (developers call such an exit a "hard fork"). Token holders can follow the exiters or remain loyal to the original core. The traditional corporate structure isn't really set up for this, so dissenting factions within a company don't really have change mechanisms at their disposal, that is, unless they can get signoff from the top brass. With a DAO, it's like cell mitosis, only with DNA that can be altered.

Some, like cryptocurrency investor Matthew McKibbin, think we'll someday be tokenizing not just tech companies, but entire cities. And serial entrepreneur David Orban thinks we'll be able to use tokenized DAOs to send a colony to Mars.

The thing about tokens is that they're category killers. They're not exactly currency, or stocks, or points in a points system. They're in some measure all of these things and yet hybridized, embedded in vast human networks. And we're still figuring them out.

How did we reach this point?

It starts quite literally in the abstract—the abstract of a 1998 paper by Alex Tabarrok. There, Tabarrok shares the outlines of what would become the private provision of public goods—that is, a solution to the classic collective-action problem:

"Many types of public goods can be produced privately by profit seeking entrepreneurs using a modified form of assurance contract, called a dominant assurance contract. I model the dominant assurance contract as a game and show that the pure strategy equilibrium has agents contributing to the public good as a dominant strategy."

If you don't speak academese, Professor Tabarrok basically spells out the crowdsourcing model in which a whole bunch of people will chip in if everyone else does. Couple that model with distributed ledgers *et voila*, you get tokenization.

"New technologies such as smart contracts and the rise of ubiquitous and massive computing power, including all manner of sensors and location technologies, may make these ideas implementable at lower cost and in better ways than ever before."[146] Tokenization, unlike taxation, enables price discovery, and you don't have to solve the free-rider problem by creating a forced-rider problem, as most contemporary politics does.

Human Fractals

Recall that above I suggested that the distributed-ledger revolution includes all technologies that have flowed from the original idea set out in the 2009 Satoshi Nakamoto white paper. By the time you read this, a hundred competitors could be vying to replace Bitcoin just in the cryptocurrency space. The point is that a distributed ledger is not just a static moment in time, but a new way of thinking about human social organization that flows forward into the future. Any number of subsequent distributed-ledger technologies may improve upon or supplant the original blockchains.

Some of the major improvements to the distributed ledger will most assuredly involve its governance. That is, how does the blockchain evolve? Does it disintermediate or hypermediate, or some of both? Does it enable collective intelligence at the level of the network or at the level of the network nodes, that is, the agents?

With disintermediation, you eliminate middlemen. The logic of the smart contract makes certain middlemen unnecessary. But this might not be the *summum bonum* of all decentralization, in all cases or at all times. As Holochain founder Arthur Brock suggests, the Bitcoin blockchain (brilliant though it may be) is nonsocial in a certain vital respect:

> In computer science, an ontology describes what EXISTS in a system. For example, in Bitcoin what exists are **transactions** organized into **blocks** linked in a chain. The first transaction in each block gets to create new **coins** (cryptographic tokens). The other transactions spend a coin by

signing (with a **private key**) the previous transaction to a new owner (using their **public key** as their address/identity). There are also **nodes** with which you send and receive transactions.

Notice no people in that ontology. They don't exist.

With no people, there are no relationships, no communication, no interconnection, no community. How can a community that doesn't exist regulate itself?[147]

Brock is not only pointing out some of the earlier weaknesses in certain applications of the blockchain. He is pointing to the idea that self-organizing systems sometimes need agents that actually exercise their agency. Sometimes we want technology to be radically *inclusive*, or, so to say, to make *everyone* potential middlemen. Call this hypermediation.

To sketch hypermediation, imagine that technology enables a system of numerous checkers. Those checkers use their minds to do the checking on the activities of others, but they themselves are checked in a kind of fractal. Each checker builds and guards a reputation so as to be considered and rewarded for future work as a checker. It's not disintermediation, but rather virtuous recursion with associated good incentives. There is no perfect human fractal, but it would still be virtuous when compared against the status quo ante.

This is *not* to argue that the original blockchain, with its logic fixed at the level of the network, isn't highly valuable for a host of use cases. Rather, there will be circumstances in which people will want to self-organize in ways that take into account their particular strengths, aptitudes, perspectives, and context. As I write, blockchain-inspired alternatives are being developed along these lines. There will be distributed ledgers for identity, reputation, and improved trust networks. And sometimes hypermediation will be required.

If human fractals work, they are likely to make decentralization even more potent, not less.

Collective Intelligence

The point of the above is not to get into the weeds of the blockchain and its children. It is rather to hint at a bright, bold future for collective intelligence and collective action.

If humans' collective intelligence is going to compete with artificial intelligence, we'd better try everything we can to find ways to build systems of programmable incentives and radical collaboration. As I suggested in the first chapter, we will eventually replace politics as the primary mechanism of societal change. This might not occur in a single moment. Rather, it's likely to be a consequence of self-organization made possible by peer-to-peer technologies.

But what is collective intelligence?

Each person has a brain and each brain, no matter how smart, has cognitive limits—strengths, weaknesses, and unique attributes. But there are ways to harness the various strengths of various brains to do things no one of those brains could come close to doing alone.

One of the first and best examples of collective intelligence is the market, according to science writer Matt Ridley. That is, "human achievements are always and everywhere collective."

> Every object and service you use is the product of different minds working together to invent or manage something that is way beyond the capacity of any individual mind. This is why central planning does not work. Ten million people eat lunch in London most days; how the heck they get what they want and when and where, given that a lot of them decide at the last minute, is baffling. Were there a London lunch commissioner to organise it, he would fail badly. Individual decisions integrated by price signals work, and work very well indeed.[148]

And prices, information wrapped in incentives, will continue to function as a primary mechanism of collective intelligence.

But novel means of collaboration and programmable incentives mean that the market mechanism gets married to the technologies of connection. "Permit these creative know-hows freely to flow," implores the narrator of Leonard Read's "I, Pencil," after explaining how innumerable workers, pursuing their own individual goals, help create it, a seemingly simple writing instrument. Busy as ants, we're building the flexible architectures of value flow around the clock.

The Limits of Collective Intelligence

We ought to be crystal clear about what we mean when we say collective intelligence, at least for the time being. CI is *not* some magical superbrain. While we should leave open the possibility that, somehow, a greater thinking noosphere can emerge from connected individuals, we have to acknowledge our current limits.

Collective intelligence "is a form of universally distributed intelligence, constantly enhanced, coordinated in real time, and resulting in the effective mobilization of skills," says cultural theorist Pierre Lévy. "I'll add the following indispensable characteristic to this definition: The basis and goal of collective intelligence is mutual recognition and enrichment of individuals rather than the cult of fetishized or hypostatized communities." In other words, Lévy is suspicious of any computerized Gaia hypothesis or magical superbrain. And we should be, too, although we should be open to new layers of the adjacent possible. Complexity could build another layer atop the noosphere.

Collective intelligence should also not be confused with group intelligence, though the latter is a subset of CI that involves small groups of people interacting effectively through brainstorming activities. Group intelligence arises in the action of, well, groups.

"We need to stop looking for leaders and start looking for teammates," admonishes complexity scientist Yaneer Bar-Yam. "We need to find others we can trust about ideas, advice, and joint action." That means turning away from both clumsy nation-state dirigisme and hermit-crab individualism.

> Society has to coalesce into local and global teams. Teams of individuals, teams of teams, and teams of teams of teams, up to society as a whole. Whether implicitly or explicitly, everybody needs to ask: Do you want to be a member of my team? Can I be a member of your team? Can we

> say "we" about ourselves to become a collective, with a collective identity?[149]

Team membership requires a different sort of decision-making and a different sort of information processing. But a teams-within-teams approach gets us closer to the most powerful kinds of CI of which humans are capable. (Recall our discussion of holacracy.)

One key to improved CI lies, therefore, in whether we can hustle ourselves into effective teams. Another lies in the speed with which teams can acquire and use information, as well as how we can further divide labor without being limited by geography or having our creative energies constrained by rigid systems. Finally, improved CI will depend on expanding the marketplace of ideas to include more and more people, while meeting them where they are. There is no magic in any of this, but instead it means building new layers of the adjacent possible through continuous improvements to networking tools, technologies and programmable incentives.

And eventually it will mean upgrading ourselves.

Heads in the Cloud

Throughout history, political theorists have played fast and loose with the term "social contract." Most of the time it's been shorthand for people taking power by claiming it is for the good of all. Justified via vague notions like Rousseau's "general will" or the where-convenient worship of that golden calf known as democracy, the hypothetical social contract has been a device through which people get their way without getting other people's actual permission.

Holonic systems—teams within teams, systems within systems—are now possible because of programmable incentives and improved CI. We also, quite literally, have a way to forge real social contracts on a global scale. This is the upgrade that could become the killer app of politics.

But wait, you might be wondering. *Don't we already have systems within systems? Teams within teams?*

Yes, but the problem is that these are scaled to the level of history and politics, not to equilibria created from free human choices for the people, by the people.

In the next chapter we'll discuss the idea of polyarchy, also known as panarchy. To ruin a punchline, this is an upgrade to our social operating system that takes polycentrism—decentralization of jurisdictions—a step further. Polyarchy offers us a way to imagine jurisdictions as being pulled away from terra firma and standing armies. It's cloud governance and thus also cloud community. Only the technology of the distributed ledger enables us to imagine that such communities are possible, maybe even inevitable.

If people have a mechanism for forging communities in the cloud, it's only a matter of time before they will. This is no truer than in those places where governance is the most broken but technology is still available to the people, such as rural Rajasthan, where villagers can upload their farms' property titles into the cloud, and Afghanistan, where women coders can take Bitcoin instead of making dangerous trips to corrupt banks. Communities of tomorrow will form entire systems of mutual aid through digital compacts that have nothing to do with borders or accidents of birth.

And so it goes. Humanity will upload important commitments into social contracts. Cosmopolitan communities of practice will form in the electronic ether. What remains on the ground—goods, services, and the relationships of flesh-and-blood neighbors—will be a far more localized phenomenon. The days of outsourcing our civic responsibilities to distant capitals are numbered.

"All things carry the yin and embrace the yang," Lao-tzu wrote. "They achieve harmony through their interaction." Thus we move headlong into the paradox of being simultaneously globalized and localized, into a more decentralized but interconnected world.

CHAPTER SIX

THE FUTURE
OF GOVERNANCE

The most radical source of
inequalities in human societies is
the "ruler-ruled" relationship. The
fashioning of a truly free world
depends upon building the
fundamental infrastructures that
enable different peoples to
become self-governing.
— Vincent Ostrom[150]

LEGAL SCHOLAR EUGEN HUBER had a big task on his hands when he
sought to unite ethnic Italians, Germans, and French under a single federal system in the early 1900s. When he succeeded, modern Switzerland was born. In
1907, the Swiss Federal Assembly passed Huber's civil code. Today the Swiss
canton system is one of the most impressive national operating systems on
earth.

It's so impressive, economist Daniel Mitchell was led to enumerate ways
"Switzerland Is Better than the United States." Following are four, according to
Mitchell:

1. The burden of government spending is lower in Switzerland. According to
    the OECD, the public sector consumes only 33.1 percent of economic out-
    put in Switzerland, compared to 41.1 percent of GDP in the United States.
2. Switzerland has genuine federalism, with the national government respon-
    sible for only about one-third of government spending. The United States
    used to be like that, but now more than two-thirds of government spending
    comes from Washington.

3. Because of a belief that individuals have a right to control information about their personal affairs, Switzerland has a strong human-rights policy that protects financial privacy. In the United States, the government can look at your bank account and does not even need a search warrant.
4. Switzerland has a positive form of multiculturalism, with people living together peacefully notwithstanding different languages and different religions. In the United States, by contrast, the government causes strife and resentment with a system of racial spoils.[151]

What makes the Swiss system so impressive with respect to point four is that it doesn't attempt to create a monolithic law or culture that demands minorities assimilate. In this way, the Swiss handle diversity far better than most countries. After all, diversity can be fracturing to a society.[152]

Switzerland isn't perfect. But it has done a pretty good job balancing diversity and unity.

More to the point, though, Switzerland has also achieved a more decentralized nation-state than the United States. In other words, the canton is as powerful as the federal government in most regards, so the Swiss are ahead of the curve.

When Huber set about weaving together the Swiss, he was concerned with updating the old Swiss Confederacy. Given Europe's intellectual and political climate at the time, this update could have been an opportunity to centralize power. One need only look at the trends in those days to see centralization was happening everywhere. Germany was consolidating power under Kaiser Wilhelm II, which helped sow the seeds of World War I. The Austro-Hungarian Empire lay close by too. The British Empire was at its height under King Edward VII. Corporatist Fascism had been spreading as an intellectual fashion in Italy.

And yet the Swiss did what the Swiss do: their own thing.

A Less Perfect Union

American-history enthusiasts will recall that Swiss-style federalism had been the basic idea behind the failed Articles of Confederation. But the revolutionaries who won American independence soon conspired to scrap the Articles after quelling a couple of rebellions of their own. The US Constitution was born. And though the Constitution is a brilliant document in most respects, creating checks and balances laterally among the branches of government, it could have done a better job of distributing power "to the states and to the people," the Ninth and Tenth Amendments notwithstanding.

The American Experiment has been, if nothing else, a wild ride. Depending on whom you ask, the US is either a beacon of hope or a Great Satan. At its inception, it was meant to be a loose confederation of states inhabited mostly by ornery farmers and a handful of fishermen. They shared a history of war, a common tongue, and some cultural similarities. Beyond that, the States were not really meant to be United.

After the Constitution had been ratified, though, Thomas Jefferson expressed concerns about America becoming a behemoth. And one of the ways he thought the US might stave off tyranny was through decentralization. In an 1800 letter to Gideon Granger, Jefferson wrote:

> Our country is too large to have all its affairs directed by a single government. Public servants at such a distance, and from under the eye of their constituents, will, from the circumstance of distance, be unable to administer and overlook all the details necessary for the good government of the citizen; and the same circumstance, by rendering detection impossible to their constituents, will invite the public agents to corruption, plunder and waste.[153]

Jefferson was always skeptical of government power, even as he wielded it. That very year, after a close election against John Adams, Jefferson became the third president of the United States. In his inaugural address he reiterated his devotion to prudent statecraft and constitutional principles and concluded that they

> should be the creed of our political faith—the text of civic instruction—the touchstone by which to try the services of those we trust; and should we wander from them in moments of error or of alarm, let us hasten to retrace our steps and to regain the road which alone leads to peace, liberty, and safety.[154]

The trouble is the US has become far too big a Leviathan, having wandered in error and alarm. It's not clear that any civic instruction could help Americans retrace their steps. For better or worse, we're on a new path.

If after a thorough reading of history, or at the very least chapter 1 of this book, you think that more centralization is largely a good thing, I probably won't be able to disabuse you of that notion. Instead I suggest plotting all the world's countries on a graph between mostly centralized (e.g. North Korea) and mostly decentralized (Switzerland). Then ask yourself: Where would you want to live?

Small (and Decentralized) is Beautiful

Switzerland isn't the only federalized country. Its neighbor Liechtenstein is a tiny nation of about 40,000 inhabitants. Though technically a monarchy, Liechtenstein is perhaps even more decentralized. Despite having a monarch as head of state, it's arguably freer, too.

In 2003, Prince Hans-Adams II presented a new constitution designed to *devolve* power. This decentralization by design meant that Liechtenstein's municipalities not only had more local authority, but could secede. In the national referendum, nearly two-thirds of voters came out in support of Hans-Adam II's new constitution, which replaced one from 1921. Few national constitutions provide a right of secession, but in Liechtenstein, all it takes is a majority vote.

"The only duties that should remain in the state's power in the third millennium are foreign policy, law and order, education and state finances,"[155] said Hans-Adams II. All remaining tasks "can be fulfilled better and cheaper on the level of communities." One might quibble with the prince about any one of these, but consider the implications of his overall claim on a country like the US. No longer would titanic debates on health-care policy occupy the national mind.

Today Liechtenstein has a corporate tax rate of 12.5 percent and an income tax rate of 1.2 percent. The smaller municipal divisions of Liechtenstein impose higher taxes for modest social welfare programs, and none taxes more than 16 percent. Could all of this decentralization have anything to do with why Liechtenstein has the highest per capita income in the world? The tiny country is of course a tax haven. But so is its neighbor Switzerland. After a certain point, we need to start looking at the rules of the game in a given country. Institutions that devolve power seem to correlate with stability and prosperity.

Planned and Grown

Above I wrote that the Swiss are "ahead of the curve." I'm referring to a curve I made up, but one that represents a real trend. In other words, central power is breaking up everywhere. Why? Because decentralization is not always a state of affairs realized through conscious planning. It is as often a process that unfolds when societies become more complex. Even Eugen Huber, weaving together three distinct legal and linguistic frameworks, was responding to both the facts of history and the pressures of modernity. But I suspect he also realized that if Switzerland went the way of the rest of Europe, it would destroy the diversity it had inherited.

When we consider China and its special economic zones (SEZs), some planned, like Shenzhen, and others grown, like Hong Kong, we see decentralization formalized by a central government. In fact, since 1958 when the total number of SEZs stood at zero percent, more than 70 percent of the world's countries now have SEZs.[156]

In other circumstances, decentralization isn't planned at all. It's a process that simply unfolds when people get frustrated in systems that are holding them back. The former colonial empires come to mind, as does the former Soviet Union after the fall of communism. People want to be free to self-determine and to try new things. Given the means, they will. On the whole, political power is moving out from central governments and down to regions, cities, and neighborhoods. And some, like technology writer Jamie Bartlett, are taking notice: "The lesson of history—real, long-lens human history—is that people move, and when they do, it's hard to stop." And it's getting easier and easier to move, writes Bartlett:

> This is the crux of the problem: nation-states rely on control. If they can't control information, crime, businesses, borders or the money supply, then they will cease to deliver what citizens demand of them. In the end, nation-states are nothing but agreed-upon myths: we give up certain freedoms in order to secure others. But if that transaction no longer works, and we stop agreeing on the myth, it ceases to have power over us.[157]

Add technology, and things get really interesting.

First, though, we have to figure our way out of an age-old conundrum, which has to do with this business of control and whether, and to what extent, we need it.

The Cooperators' Dilemma

For the last 5,000 years or so, humanity has been caught in a kind of trap. To cooperate, we have had to trust each other. Not everyone can be trusted, though. Our counterparts might try to take advantage. So cooperation has depended on trusting the biggest intermediary of all, government, to make sure people play nice and predatory behavior gets suppressed. Enforcing rules and suppressing predators takes power.

But we can't always trust intermediaries. They sometimes try to take advantage of us, too. The power used to enforce can be used to dominate through coercion, so the distinction between enforcer and predator can get blurry. And yet we've had to trust people with power to do their jobs, despite the fact that there is rarely a superordinate power to check them. If there were such a power, we'd need an even more powerful enforcer to check the superordinate power. And on it goes—unless we figure out a way for government to control itself.

Let's call it Madison's Paradox after the American founder who wrote:

> In framing a government which is to be administered by men over men, the great difficulty lies in this: you must first enable the government to control the governed; and in the next place oblige it to control itself. A dependence on the people is, no doubt, the primary control on the government; but experience has taught mankind the necessity of auxiliary precautions.[158]

Madison's prescription was to segment power and set it upon itself in a kind of wasteful competition. And yet this counterintuitive operating system was better than any world had seen. It constrained power in a novel way. But it was not perfect. Republican constitutions have given rise to factions in countries, such as the US, where they have been adopted. Power thus ends up on the auction block for well-connected favor seekers. So even if we oblige government to control itself, it doesn't always work out so well. Political power tends to feed itself. And it grows through mechanisms of debt, taxation, or special-interest capture. When these mechanisms are combined, rolling back power be-comes nigh impossible.

Under this modern conception of power, which almost everyone accepts, justice remains something that must be both stewarded and meted out by the powerful. So wisdom, according to those who hold power, has always been about finding the right distribution of rewards and punishments. Sprinkle in a little virtue from time to time if you can. If you get big enough, you're delegating power to subordinates who must in turn distribute rewards and punishments.

James Madison's brilliance was to turn such wisdom into a system of checks and balances, with rewards and punishments applied among the powerful, too. As brilliant as that system has been, power finds a way. Little by little, govern-ment as a steward of justice, if it ever was, has given way to the state as an ap-paratus of self-propagating power. So what are we to do? Is Madison's Paradox an inescapable aspect of the human condition? Must we continue to trust people with power to serve as intermediaries and hope they won't be or become preda-tors? Or is there another way?

The Fact of Pluralism

Before we return to the questions before us, let's acknowledge something that rarely gets acknowledged. People are different, one from the next. Groups are different, one from the next. It's not just that I like vanilla ice cream and you like chocolate, it's also that we have different conceptions of value and differ-ent ideas about the good life.

The fact of pluralism has deep implications for the vital questions of gover-nance. Whose conception of justice are we to enforce? What if our conceptions come into conflict? Are there any human universals at all? And if so, how are we to find them? If pluralism is a fact and we indeed hold different values, maybe we can upgrade our social operating systems to accommodate these dif-ferences. Doing so will require a change of perspective on the question of cen-tral authority.

At this point, it's tempting to launch into philosophical debates about the bounds of pluralism, but as we enter the post-ideological era, we will experi-ence a force more powerful than first principles or fires in the mind: market competition.

This is not to argue that voice isn't still vitally important to the functioning of any social order. Myriad governance options will mean, in some sense, that voice will be just as important as ever. As we reorganize ourselves into communities that reflect our particular conceptions of the good, we will exercise voice locally. And all systems old and new will have to adapt to changing circumstances, while trying to attract and retain people.

That means, if we are able, we will live in different systems and play by different rules. In fact, we tend to cluster with people who share our values, whatever they might be. And aside from politeness through gritted teeth at family dinners, we don't in general move in the same circles as those with whom we disagree. And though some might claim that people of other political persuasions are backwards or crazy, we should be as tolerant and charitable as possible.

Reflection, Revolution, and Evolution

The ideas we are about to explore lie on a spectrum between ideology and evolution, which makes for a delicate dance. That is, we're used to thinking in terms of how we believe things ought to be (ideology), but we're pushing the slider towards how we think things can and will develop (evolution). Thus our thinking requires a mix of "is" and "ought" that some might not be comfortable with. For example, pluralism is a state of affairs—an outcome we'll have to live with. And yet it is an outcome we should *want* to live with. So we're arguing both that pluralism is likely to happen due to contemporary circumstances and that we want to actively catalyze it. Such thinking requires both the reflection of a philosopher and the alertness of an entrepreneur.

Polycentrism and Competitive Governance

It seems like decentralization is a good thing. But how do we know? And whose idea of what's good are we talking about? If we accept the fact of pluralism, the answer to the latter question is: it depends. Decentralizing authority in some territory, say, involves trade-offs to be sure. If we think about decentralization as representing exit options, it means there are simply more places to go if you don't like how things are done where you are. So people can choose to live in systems that are closer to their respective ideals. To unpack this idea a little more, let's use our imaginations.

Suppose you are an American. (For this thought experiment, you don't have to gain weight or carry a gun.) Let's also imagine that you have the choice of living in either of two neighboring states: New Hampshire and Vermont. People in these two states tend to have very different governance philosophies. Now, the Amendment Fairy comes and changes the system overnight. With a wave of her wand, the fairy has done away with most of the federal government—Liechtenstein style. Now, you're basically living in one of two different smaller countries: New Hampshire or Vermont. Which one do you choose?

If you choose New Hampshire, you'll live in a condition of low taxes, low regulation, and robust entrepreneurship. You'll obtain health insurance and purchase medical care privately in a price-competitive environment. In short, after shedding federal law, New Hampshire becomes a radically free market. If you choose Vermont, you'll have higher taxes and more regulation, which might make starting a business more difficult. But you will have a bigger social safety net, and government will provide certain goods and services such as health care. After shedding federal law, Vermont becomes democratic socialist.

Picked your state yet?

Seeing things through the lens of competitive governance, we're not concerned with which option is better. We're concerned with the idea that these two different options exist at all. In fact, we can extend our thought experiment to forty-eight other states, each of which can be subdivided into cities and counties. We might be able to convince you that all these choices are a good thing. After all, whichever state you're in, you have forty-nine others that might offer the chance of living in a system that is better suited to your preferences.

Here's the thing, though: a loose confederation of more diverse states doesn't mean anything goes. Authoritative forces constrain each state's system: competition and fiscal reality. In other words, your system has to be able to attract and retain real people, and it has to do so without breaking the bank.

In this way, each state (or city-state) can determine its own governance and mix of public and private provision of goods. But it will have to do so like a business. If you don't do things wisely, your best and brightest will leave for your neighboring jurisdiction, and there's nothing you can do about that. Get your stuff together or suffer an exodus. Such a polycentric order will continuously self-equilibrate, with the parameters of utopian thinking set by reality. Competitors in the governance market can no longer treat people as mere subjects or citizens. They have to treat them like customers.

In this way, polycentrism represents the death of political theory. Experimenta-tion, competition, and evolutionary change have little to do with the fires of ideology. If you're an ideologue in a polycentric order, you have to test your theory in the petri dish of competition. Now, maybe you think polycentrism is itself an ideology. You might even argue that the very thought is beyond the pale. But if you're open to the idea that systems can and should compete, we all might be able to get that much closer to our ideals.

According to Joe Quirk of the Seasteading Institute, the way to get good gov-ernment is to treat governance like startups. "Seasteading is less an ideology than a technology," he says. "Among the dozen or so full-time people who have worked on our staff at the Seasteading Institute since 2008 are folks who have identified as conservative, progressive, libertarian, and confused. All of us worked side by side straight through two national US elections and barely men-tioned them." That's because seasteaders share a common perspective: we need "more experiments in governance" and "start-ups are the way to discover solu-tions." You'll often see Quirk and company wearing T-shirts that read "Stop Ar-guing, Start Seasteading."[159]

Whether on sea or land, people are enormously creative. Decentralization af-fords people the opportunity to try new systems of governance and migrate among them. It is an industry.

"An extremely useful way to think about the incentives that structure the politi-cal game is to consider the market for governance," write seasteading scholars Brad Taylor and Patri Friedman. "Rules have economic value, and people would be willing to pay for them. We can think of the bundle of rules and pub-lic goods provided by government as a product, governments as producers, citi-zens as consumers, and taxes as prices."[160]

Competition among governments functions rather like competition among op-erating systems. And though there will be network effects, making the switch could someday be as simple as migrating from iOS to Android.

What's So Great about Polycentrism?

Not everyone intuitively recognizes that competition among governance rule sets is a good thing. So it behooves us to share at least one practical thing about polycentrism at the outset: antifragility. Nassim Nicholas Taleb sets out an en-tire theory in his book *Antifragile*, but the basic idea is that no one element of a system should be so essential that if it fails, the entire system does too. Inevitably, claims Taleb, black swans or hubristic rulers will come along and threaten monolithic systems. Distributing or decentralizing systems—including governance systems—makes them less vulnerable or more "antifragile".

"If there is something in nature you don't understand," Taleb cautions,

> odds are it makes sense in a deeper way that is beyond your understanding. So there is a logic to natural things that is much superior to our own. Just as there is a dichotomy in law: "innocent until proven guilty" as opposed to "guilty until proven innocent," let me express my rule as follows: what Mother Nature does is rigorous until proven otherwise; what humans and science do is flawed until proven otherwise.[161]

This rule of thumb is as important for human interactions, as we have to design tools and rules around what humans are, rather than what we wish them to be.

In similar fashion, polycentricity is biomimicry. To mimic nature, we can start by privileging law that emerges from the natural interactions and collisions of people moving about in the world. The common law, for example, has evolved over time. Statutes, by contrast, are rationalist contrivances of central elites. Still, if central elites are to design law to some degree (as Eugen Huber did), they will do well to practice "network design," which means good protocols for free agents flowing within antifragile systems.

"Design harnesses the designer's subconscious, and it recognizes the need to empathize with the user's," explains complexity theorist Diego Espinosa. "Of course, it isn't as black and white as all that, but rather a matter of orientation. Design largely bypasses the Cartesian payoffs-and-probabilities calculus. It embraces human fallibility and the chance to learn from error. It goes where complexity takes it."[162]

The question before us, then, is: Where will complexity take us next?

Polyarchy

Only the savviest readers will have noticed a big, fat assumption packaged into the conversation so far. Recall the idea of "neighboring" states. If you don't like

Vermont, we said, you can move to New Hampshire. This framing, though thoroughly ingrained in our thinking, might increasingly be unnecessary. It's an artifact of human history since the dawn of agriculture. It's a byproduct of war, conquest, and the drawing of borders upon territory.

In *Polystate,* cartoonist Zach Weinersmith argues that, whether in Catalonia or Texas, the imposition of the "geostate" (governing laws) upon the "anthrostate" (emergent culture) can never simply be taken for granted. That is, "a geostate continues to be itself only so long as there is not a discrete moment at which the people governed by it choose for it to change, usually at great cost of blood, treasure, and order." The connection among people, territory, and law is thus contingent. "Geostates are not pre-ordained by the human condition. They should not be taken as inevitable. We should especially consider the extent to which technology influences the meaning of geography."[163]

Indeed. What if we realized most of what counts as jurisdiction today is completely arbitrary? What if most of what falls under the rubric of governance today need not be tied to territory at all?

Most people are political partisans if they care about such matters at all. If you're a partisan, I have a challenge for you: Have you dreamed of a day when your favored party could finally implement every plank in its platform? Seriously. What if it were possible? What if you could live in your favorite system of government—and keep all those idiots in that other party from obstructing your plans? One such proposal recommends itself.

"In the past and in the present, the idea of tailoring the experience of every individual to his taxes, healthcare laws, social services, and so on would be unthinkable," writes Weinersmith. "Government bureaucracy is large enough without having to provide this massive service. But suppose that at some point, computer AI is good enough that 'computer assistants' actually assist the user in a meaningful way? Suppose that more and more delivery of goods and services can be done on the spot by individuals, thanks to better technology? In this case, it is possible that government could be extremely tailored to the individual."[164]

Computer assistants are one thing. Amazon is another. But people have been kicking around similar ideas since well before Ray Kurzweil and Jeff Bezos.

The Great Partisan Challenge[165]

Let's go back in time—to Belgium. It's 1860.

A liberal thinker named Paul-Emile de Puydt proposed our great partisan challenge more than 150 years ago in a dialogue of sorts. De Puydt wrote:

> In each community a new office is opened, a "Bureau of Political Membership." This office would send every responsible citizen a declaration form to fill in. . . .
>
> Question: What form of government would you desire?
>
> Quite freely you would answer, monarchy, or democracy, or any other. . . .
>
> Anyway, whatever your reply, your answer would be entered in a register arranged for this purpose; and once registered, unless you withdrew your declaration, observing due legal form and process, you would thereby become either a royal subject or citizen of the republic. . . .
>
> Ultimately, everyone would live in his own individual political community, quite as if there were not another, nay, ten other, political communities nearby, each having its own contributors too.[166]

See the challenge?

In short: You can live under any political system you like without leaving your driveway. Instead of joining a party, you join a political association and agree to live under its auspices—rules that track with your sense of the right and the good. A real "social contract." The only cost of this leap forward is this: You cannot force anyone to join your chosen association.

So, would you do it? If not, why not?

Could it be that you're concerned about how people would resolve disagreements? De Puydt writes:

> If a disagreement came about between subjects of different governments, or between one government and a subject of another, it would simply be a matter of observing the principles hitherto observed between neighboring peaceful States; and if a gap were found, it could be filled without difficulties by [appeal to] human rights and all other possible rights. Anything else would be the business of ordinary courts of justice.

While we might agree that "human rights" is an ambiguous term, we can assume, given de Puydt's classical-liberal commitments, that he means people should be protected from involuntary servitude.

Maybe you're worried that all the rich people would flee your chosen association or form their own association—like Liechtenstein—leaving less-wealthy, less-greedy members of your association to care for the poor. Wealthy people can already leave their jurisdictions (and some, like Facebook investor Eduardo Savarin, do). But most do not. If the voting patterns of the wealthy are any indication, plenty of rich people in America tolerate higher taxation rates and support government systems intended to help the poor. Those who don't support these policies overwhelmingly believe that delivering aid to the poor through government programs is particularly ineffective or inhumane; while they oppose state welfare, it isn't because they have no interest in relieving distress.

In any case, why not let the best system win?

What about common interests affecting all the inhabitants of a certain area—whatever their political allegiances? De Puydt thinks "each government, in this case, would stand in relation to the whole nation roughly as each of the Swiss cantons . . . stand in relation to their federal government."

I would add that such "issues" must be linked specifically to territory. That is, most issues addressed by national governments are not relevant to questions of territory per se, but are laws attached to history's contingencies—for example, to national boundaries drawn after the ends of wars. In other words, if officials in Washington, DC, get to decide which health-care system you live under, that is probably because your mother gave birth to you on a certain patch of soil. De Puydt's panarchy helps us to shed that arbitrariness.

Still have concerns? Whatever your objection to de Puydt's challenge, is it so great that you're willing to continue in this wasteful, unsatisfying game of partisan tug-of-war? Are you so blinkered by status quo bias that you just can't imagine people choosing their political associations and living by their own rules? Or does your bias boil down to the idea that your political preferences are best, so you think your political party should dominate all others? It's not like there's much good in the blur of politics.

Democracy is a system that leaves us all at the whim of mob rule. It may be formalized mob rule—and that mob has to share power with representatives captured by corporate interests. But at the very least de Puydt's proposal should prompt us to think about what kinds of human social arrangements are possible beyond democracy.

If you're opening your mind to de Puydt's proposal, you have come a long way. And if you have taken the challenge and come out on the other side convinced, then you are probably ready to upgrade from the Democratic Operating System. Under America's DOS you have two apps. And that's not much of a choice for anyone these days. In European countries, there are a few more apps, but they're buggy too.

Wouldn't it be better if politics were more like choosing from apps on a tablet —with infinite choices and, if you're savvy enough, the option to start a new one? It seems we're stuck in a social technology that no longer makes sense. Democracy is not a system designed to grant us our political wishes. It is a system in which others' preferences get clustered together, bizarrely, as a feature of the system. And the rules we have to live under are arbitrary with respect to our real political preferences.

When you enter a voting booth, you might as well be sending your prayers up to Washington, DC. But how many times do those prayers get answered? Even if your guy gets elected, he doesn't give you the policies you'd like to see. Hardly anyone is happy with the sausage that gets produced in our legislatures. Only an ignoramus who thinks of politics as a kind of team sport is happy six months after Election Day, whether she wears a red or a blue jersey.

Belgian statesman Charles de Brouckère commented, just before his death:

> De Puydt [has furnished] an outline of a system that would
> have the advantage of submitting the industry of security

> production, otherwise known as governments, to a competi-
> tion as complete as that in which manufacturers of fabrics,
> for example, engage in a country under free trade, and
> achieves this without having recourse to revolutions, barri-
> cades, or even the smallest act of violence.[167]

If democracy is a way of transferring power without bullets, de Puydt's "panarchy" is a way of truly distributing power among the people. Here's de Brouckère again:

> If society were to adopt the system proposed by M. de
> Puydt, each citizen would be able change governments at
> least as easily as a tenant changes furnished apartments in a
> large city; because he would need to commit himself for
> only one year to follow the laws of the government of his
> choice and to defray expenses at rates discussed in advance.
> At the end of this year's trial, the citizen would be free to
> subscribe, for his consumption of security and other public
> services, to the establishment that produced these things in
> the manner most congruent with his tastes and for the
> amount that he desires to devote to this expense.[168]

Instead of a game in which the red team and blue team fight over who gets to
make and enforce the rules, why don't we have an honest competition in which
associations compete for members by offering better systems with better rules
—as determined by those members?

The next time you hear someone carelessly toss out a reference to the "social
contract," offer de Puydt's challenge. If nothing else, it is an interesting way to
infuriate your in-laws and social-media contacts. (Notice the similarities between de Puydt's system and social media.) With this challenge, we can go a
long way in exposing the fact that politics is just another sort of religion—a belief system that is fundamentally about forcing others to live exactly the way
we want them to. (That's so twentieth century.)

Still some may not be satisfied with this challenge. And, those unsatisfied by
the idea will find they want to go deeper. So let's test the idea a little more.

Challenging the Centralist

Academic George Lakoff once compared taxation to paying membership dues at a club. Steven Pinker gave him a hard time for it, and deservedly so. After all, if you don't pay your taxes "men with guns will put you in jail."[169] But what if that didn't happen? What if we accept the best of Lakoff's mendacious metaphor and downgraded citizenship to membership in a community?

To be fair, we're still at the theoretical stage. But before I offer my uncomplicated ideas for social change, I want to present a challenge to the centralist—that is, to anyone who believes that government power is good, that it makes the world better than it would otherwise be, and that governments should have monopolies over certain goods, services, and spheres of activity.

Most people agree you have the right to leave the county, state, or country if you don't like what the government in that jurisdiction has handed down. You can go live somewhere else, though probably under a different thumb or set of thumbs. What do our systems of justice—determined by something as arbitrary as geography—demand of us? Do we have a right of exit?

For the centralist there seem to be two possible responses:

X. If you can put your hands on someone to govern them, that is, on her body and/or her wealth, whether in Sweden, or a secret island, you would be justified. There is really some objective, global justice the ends of which justify your means of getting to her; or

Y. Considerations of pragmatics and citizenship mean that once someone is in another jurisdiction, so long as she hasn't broken any laws in your jurisdiction, she is no longer your concern. Because she is living in another place, under different rules, you have no right to bother her there now—whatever your concept of justice.

I think fair-minded centralists will stick to Y. Those committed to X are the ones with whom we may eventually have to think of ourselves as being at war. Still, those who'd answer X live among us. But I think those that lean towards Y might be persuaded about a right of *ultimate* exit. Indeed, if we can exploit a problem with Y—call it territorial chauvinism—we might be able to make good headway with our case.

To the point: By virtue of *what*, exactly, does my living in some geography require my compliance with a single system encompassing some bundle of goods and services provided by the state? Why can't I become a member of a Swiss-, Singaporean-, or Swedish-style system of administration? If your answer is "because you live in this system, not in another" you're arguing in a circle. I'm trying to find out what it is about my living—geographically—within a given system that makes me duty bound?

One fair answer might be that there are *functions* of the state that are more or less linked to territory. We enjoy these functions just because we live in an area. But which ones? Let's pull out the government functions that relate to the territory where one lives and focus on those. In the interests of convincing you that I'm not crazy, I won't get all anarchist and suggest privatizing everything under the sun. I want only to introduce a thought experiment that is charitable to the idea of so-called "public" benefits while recognizing only the ones that people would enjoy *by virtue of living somewhere*.

Consider the following list of territorial goods:

1. Transportation and roads
2. National defense
3. Emergency services
4. Justice and local dispute resolution
5. Utilities and waste disposal
6. Prisons
7. Parks and aesthetics
8. Nuisance court or zoning
9. Environment and waste disposal
10. Identification and immigration

For the sake of discussion, I'm simply granting that territorial goods have an inherent *publicness* about them. Some might argue, for example, that police and defense should be considered territorial goods because it's easier to free ride on others who pay for these. In other words, I'll benefit from national-defense spending even if I don't pay for it. Or, if security patrols are walking your neighborhood, you'll benefit even if your neighbors pay and you don't. There are other goods, like dispute resolution and property rights, that establish not only the "operating system" for a territory but standards and legal precedents the law provides generally. It may turn out that some or even all of these territorial goods would be better provided by private companies. But let's agree that the above list can be considered territorial goods, even though an anarchist would want to privatize or abolish them and an economist would not call them all "public goods." (In economics, a "public good" is one that you can't provide to some and not others and that is no less available to one person because another is using it too.[170])

All other goods and services, such as health insurance, education, and art aren't really linked to territory. I can enjoy the benefits of health-insurance risk pooling and online education virtually anywhere I live. While I may benefit from a tax-supported theater in my area, it is arguably not something that everyone needs or uses—like roads or first responders. Nor are these services public goods in the economic sense. That is, consuming them means someone else can't. And it might be easy to identify who's using these goods and charge them for it.

And that brings us back to an important question: if I'm OK with your leaving the US and becoming a citizen of Sweden, or leaving New York and becoming a resident of North Carolina, why shouldn't I be OK with your right of exit from *any* nonterritorial system? If there is nothing intrinsically territorial about a system that provides goods and services like health care or education in a certain way, why ought I not simply be allowed to "exit" without moving to a different system's territory?

Rules of Polyarchy

Increasingly it will be more apparent to people that we should separate nonterritorial systems from territorial systems of goods. With technological progress, people are going to demand greater latitude to form nonterritorial systems *across geographies* based on individual interests and beliefs. Of course, the devil is in the implementation. But the idea is straightforward: it's time we divorced nonterritorial systems of goods from territorial systems.

But how would this work?

It would take two fairly simple changes to the law of the land. That is, two new rules. These new rules would track with the two different types of goods systems we touched on. Let's call the nonterritorial systems "communities" and the territorial systems "territories." For communities we have a right of exit. For territories, we have a rule of localization.

A right of exit means:

> Anyone can leave a community at any time as long as he or
> she has honored his or her end of any membership agree-
> ment.

You can be a member of any community you like. Membership in that community can have all sorts of provisions and conditions, but you can always disasso-
ciate yourself from any community you have joined. You can take all the resources you were once required to pay in taxes and use them for resources to
pay for anything—including your membership in another community (or multiple other communities). It's that simple. You may prefer the rugged life outside
of any community. From my point of view, that would be unwise, but it would
be your right.

Communities, which we've defined here as systems of allocating or exchanging
nonterritorial goods or services, can be highly diverse. With a right of exit, we
have the possibility to unleash the creative forces of competition. Some of these
communities might be based on the areas in which we live, but many would exist across territories. With no territory responsible for the provision of, say,
health care or income support, I might join a cooperative that pools risk across
all the members to create some form of social insurance.

In this health-care system, maybe only a certain number of people with poor
health or existing conditions would be allowed to join, maybe not. As a condition of membership, I might also be required to pay for certain coverage items.
Of course, this system would compete with other health-care communities for
members. A competitor might require its members, say, to put a certain amount
of money each month into a personal health savings account. But membership
might also cost less with such an arrangement. Either way, it would be impossible to force others to join my chosen system. Instead, I could join the health-
care system I thought was the most efficient, the most effective, or even the
most morally upright.

No health system would depend for its existence upon everyone in some geography being forced to join. It would, rather, be an issue of individual preference
and ethical bent. While market forces would constrain the form and feasibility
of any system, the system need not be "free market" as narrowly defined. One
could opt into a communal arrangement just as easily as she could opt into a

patient-driven model. And we would consider that her right as a sovereign human being.

Who knows whether communities would evolve to look anything like our contemporary political caricatures of Democrats and Republicans, Labour and Conservative. People might cluster in all sorts of ways we cannot anticipate. With different incentives and competition among communities, even the most "progressive" person might come to see the world differently. The staunchest individualist might find new social ventures for which he couldn't resist volunteering. King-of-the-mountain politics simply wouldn't be much a part of this new country, but moral suasion and marketing would most surely be.

Economic philosopher Deirdre McCloskey calls it "sweet talk":

> Does persuasive economic talk have economic significance? Yes. One can show on the basis of detailed occupational statistics for the U.S. that about a quarter of income in a modern economy is earned by "sweet talk"—not lies or trickery always, but mainly the honest persuasion that a manager must exercise in a society of free workers or that a teacher must exercise to persuade her students to read books or that a lawyer must exercise if a society of laws is [to] be meaningful. The economy values sweet talk at one quarter of its total income, a gigantic and economically meaningful sum.[171]

To get more sweet talk, we would have to introduce new rules. Then, people can put their money where their mouths are.

Some readers will be concerned about moral relativism. And I have to admit that polyarchy includes some. After all, a community might require pretty much anything you can imagine as a condition of membership. One community might want people to cluster together, as in Amish communities or on kibbutzim. Another community might be as cosmopolitan as you please, with members worldwide connected electronically. Communities could restrict members' behavior in ways most of us would find crazy, but since those restrictions would only apply to members, no one would be bound who didn't agree. Of course, I hesitate to say that memberships would entail people getting to kill each other for either minor contract violations or fun. The point of this thought experiment is *not* to test the bounds of which communities we would consider extreme cases. That's a discussion for another day. Barring the hard cases, the result would approach maximum pluralism. But not chaos.

What about territorial systems?

If we assume that such systems are justified due to their association with territorial goods, we can employ a localization rule to keep all authority for such systems as near to the action as possible:

> Legitimate governance functions should be handled at the most local level feasible.

The idea is that the smaller the territory, the more likely you are to approach unanimity. In the absence of such unanimity, it is at least that much easier for people to move to a territory they find tolerable. When any task or administrative function is carried out at the most local level feasible, a state government, for example, would never deal with roads if counties could, and so on. Of course, as a corollary to our rule of localization, we might also want to set the area of a basic territory, initially. After all, we would want to draw territorial boundaries in such a way that it's easy enough to move out, but large enough to get economies of scale. If a certain task, such as building regional highways or defending against invaders, required wider geography, then our localization rule would give the authority to handle that task to a system with wider territorial boundaries. Compared to what we have currently, there would be a lot less authority in large jurisdictions, and a lot more in small ones.

Decentralization and local empowerment would follow these rule changes. A federal government might end up having responsibility for an extremely narrow set of goods, such as defense and a court of ultimate arbitration (a supreme court of sorts). Otherwise, you'd have the common law and probably no legislatures outside of territorial boards or councils. It's not clear at this point what larger regional provinces or states would have responsibility for, if they needed to exist at all. Provinces might handle disputes among territories or be responsible for planning and coordinating certain emergency functions that territories couldn't handle. They might deal with the administration of interterritorial highway projects. The common law would handle most environmental problems.

Financing Polyarchy

If governance communities require resources to work, they will charge fees. Some will offer different fees for different people based on ability to pay. Others will use different models, and presumably the models people like best will be the ones that win out.

At the regional or national level, it might be that these superordinate jurisdictions have to tax. It could be a land-value tax or a sales tax. Or it might be that these higher levels charge the various smaller territories or their members fees for services directly involving them. A number of models recommend themselves, so we needn't be doctrinaire. Taxes or fees would likely be relatively low in territories that dealt only with police, defense, and territorial justice, particularly given competition from neighboring territories. And that isn't merely theoretical. In the US, residents have fled from high-tax states such as California to low-tax states such as Texas.[172]

If a territory provided territorial goods and services that citizens really liked, they might be willing to stay and pay more in taxes. That is much easier to determine locally than nationally. Sound roads and attractive thoroughfares are local. Major highways are perhaps not. Again, relative limits on the size of a territory and its functions—due not only to localization but to tax competition among territories—ought to keep taxes reasonably low. Experimentation in both revenue collection and provision of these localized goods would allow territories to try approaches that could then be copied or scrapped. In short, lower fees and higher quality of services would be far more likely to follow in an environment of competitive governance.

One might be persuaded that all these services can be provided privately and, in the interests of justice, ought to be. Let the experiments begin. I will leave our simple rules, a right of exit and localization, as a happy medium between the status quo and anarchy. We need not settle ideological disputes here. Rather, we can experiment with solutions to problems that crop up if we fail to innovate in the area of governance.

Organic Unity

Before we get into the deeper question of political justice, let's indulge in a detour for a moment. In his great work *Philosophical Explanations*, Robert Nozick invites us to consider the idea of organic unity. The idea, roughly, is that within any system there is value in the balance of diversity and unity, whether in systems of art, science, or society. Maybe Nozick was inspired by the dollar bill dictum "e pluribus unum" (out of many, one). Nozick might also have offered "ex uno plures" (out of one, many). Either way, diversity and unity were mutually constraining, according to Nozick—a sweet spot of value. "Can we draw a curve of degree of organic unity with the two axes being degree of diversity and degree of unifiedness?" asked Nozick. The diversity axis will constrain the unity axis and vice versa so that both achieve a kind of stasis. The beauty of Nozick's graph, apart from its simplicity, is its appeal to some intuitive notion of balance.

Why would any such notion be important to our idea of society? Of course, when we are unified we are at peace. But again, pluralism means people with different conceptions of happiness and the good life can coexist. Organizing society is not about finding a singular ideal to be crafted by central masterminds. Rather, it is as about acknowledging our differences, accepting them as a fact of life, and unleashing the creative forces that arise from those differences.

Pulling Together

But does the common acceptance of pluralism unite us, too? Are there any other unifying forces?

I might once have said "the rule of law." Sadly, that phrase has been perverted by opportunists who simply want to pass laws, which rather misses the point. That a bill gets through a legislative sausage grinder does not make said bill right, good, and prudent. To comport with a rule-of-law framework, a law should apply equally to everyone and privilege no person or group.

But there again, polyarchy—properly implemented—might include corrupt or autocratic jurisdictions for a time. My hypothesis, however, is that corruption can't long survive when the cost of exit is low. The governance market's evolutionary forces would supply de facto rule of law. So under our proposed system, things would be clearer and simpler. The effect of our two simple rules would amount to a massive reboot, complete with a new social operating system. We would end up dismantling the big, old, Byzantine edifice of federal and state legislation and replacing it with new, bottom-up bodies of rules established by communities and territories bound by their commitment to a couple of basic rules and the value of toleration.

Maybe at the core of all this, we could build in a rule that people should be harmed as little as humanly possible, as variations on this rule, if not timeless, keep cropping up over time. The Buddhist's ahimsa. Mill's harm principle. Hillel the Elder's golden rule. If there is a central anything, a general prohibition on violence, theft, and fraud could take us far in establishing a social system that yields peace, prosperity, and pluralism.

In the US Declaration of Independence, the object of reverence was once our unalienable rights to "Life, Liberty and the pursuit of Happiness." In the American Constitution, there are the enumerated and unenumerated rights. And while we may quibble over the philosophical origins of so-called "natural rights," writing down the principles of a people has powerful connotations upon which a culture may be developed. And a culture of peace is essential to the survival of any formal institutions that enshrine rights.

It used to be that rights talk was a way to establish anti-authoritarian culture and social coherence. In revolutionary times it was a leading indicator of change. Whether in pamphleteering by a Tom Paine or in the Constitution, Americans had formed a kind of secular religion. Likewise, an institution of universalistic justice built on some principle of nonharm could provide both a legal guide for ultimate dispute resolution and a symbol worthy of our reverence. But contemporary circumstances militate against the idea that such culture is enough. Human freedom must be hacked. Rights and freedoms will be an epiphenomenon of human choices, not something doled out by ostensibly wise elites.

If there is a unifying aspect to future societies, maybe some body of ultimate arbitration or adjudication will evolve. And yet we have to be realistic about intellectual fashions, including those we hold most dear. Polyarchy stops short of any doctrinaire embrace of ideology. It's really more about rules of thumb for governance entrepreneurs seeking to attract customers to their services.

Legal scholar Tom W. Bell identifies six best practices for governance, for example. Whether these emerge ex post or are planned ex ante, Bell thinks the following are critical:

1. Respect for consent
2. Protection of fundamental rights
3. Independent adjudication
4. Clear and fair interpretive rules

5. Remedies for wrongs
6. Freedom of exit[173]

Let us be under no illusions: there will never again be a constitutional moment. The enlightenment project is moribund. So if there is no unifying third super-rule, we will be unified by whatever equilibrium gets forged in the evolutionary fires of the market in governance.

Plenty of places for caveats exist in all of this. But I hope two rules and a principle are enough for a good start to an important conversation. In the search for rules that maximize the number of possible communities available for people to join voluntarily, a right of exit and a rule of localization would take us very far indeed. While these rules would not be perfect, nor make us perfectly free, they would represent a giant move away from the status quo. These rules would mean a leap towards a thousand intentional communities. Experimentation would enable the flourishing of all kinds of systems—all of which would work toward the balance of each member's ideas of peace, security, abundance, and personal sovereignty. By joining communities, we could still indulge some of our most clannish human instincts.

Localization and a right of exit are likely to be the products not of deliberative bodies but of new circumstances that emerge as we approach the social singularity.

Robert Nozick, in his seminal *Anarchy, State, and Utopia*, writes of a utopia of utopias, which offers the theoretical basis for our vision of the future. Each utopia, or "pattern of community" will have to be tried out. "Some communities will be abandoned, others will struggle along, others will split, others will flourish, gain members, and be duplicated elsewhere. Each community must win and hold the voluntary adherence of its members."[174]

The only cost of this system would be never being able to indulge the urge to dominate others for the sake of a single great utopia. And though the totality of our systems of governance might look like holons, systems within systems, the purveyors of those systems would be answerable to us. Persuasion finally would rule over power.

Frontiers of Governance

I hope by this point you have seen just how deep the rabbit hole goes. We're just warming up, dear reader. The rabbit hole goes much deeper, especially if we drop in a dash of technology and stir. If you are persuaded by any of the foregoing as a theoretical construct, there are practical applications, old and new, that are likely to demonstrate just how we can form associations in the cloud. *We shape our tools, and then our tools shape us. We shape our rules, and then our rules shape us.*

At the risk of dissolving everything I've written up to this point, we should return to a point we gave short shrift above: Not all decentralization is designed. Even the theoretical examples of polyarchy set out above seem to labor under the idea of a legal framework designed by elites. But decentralization in the age of complexity is already bursting forth from the technologies of interaction created by subversive innovators.

Even though there is no unclaimed dirt left to settle, human freedom and human community are about to enjoy a renaissance.

Invisible Cities

Imagine we're standing on a ridge. We look out on a valley awash in sunlight, surveyors contemplating a new city. We squint and ask: What will it look like? Will it have its own rules, culture, and commercial life? Will it be a bustling metropolis or a constellation of villages?

The Internet has only been part of everyday life for about twenty years. If the Northwest Ordinance and the Homestead Acts were legal sanction for expansion across the American continent, networking technologies are invitations for people both to spread out and to connect with others in novel ways. This opportunity has important implications.

For much of history, we have thought of the law and the land as being inseparable, particularly as the conquerors were often the lawgivers. Not anymore. For the first time, jurisdiction and territory can be separated to a great degree, thanks to innovation.

So many of the administrative functions of jurisdiction can increasingly be found in the cloud. It's early, yes. The network is fragile. But we will soon be able to pass in and out of legal systems, selecting those that benefit us, employing true self-government. It is time to follow Thoreau, who, in *Civil Disobedience*, asked, "Is a democracy, such as we know it, the last improvement possible in government?"

Already, we can buy and sell using cryptocurrencies. We are programming the incentives of tomorrow's companies. These are just the first brushfires of a new form of social coordination in which technology *itself* makes it possible to upgrade our social operating systems.

Peer-to-peer interaction means we're a nation of joiners again—on steroids. It seemed for a while we had lost the republic to special interests. But the hopeless calculus of cronyism—concentrated benefits and dispersed costs—is being flipped on its head. Networking technology makes it so we're enjoying the fruits of the sharing economy—quite rapidly, in fact. Cronies and officials are finding it hard to play catch up.

New constituencies are forming around these new benefits. Special interests that once squeaked to get the oil are confronted by battalions bearing smartphones. Citizens, fed up with leaving their prayers in the voting booth, are voting more with their dollars and their devices. Free association is now ensured by design, not by statute.

Technology that changes incentives can change institutions. The rules and regulations we currently live under came out of DOS. It used to be that these institutions shaped our incentives to a great degree. Now we have ways of coordinating our activities that obviate state intermediaries, corporate parasites, and moribund laws.

And this change isn't just the stuff of theory. People are putting the principles of distributed power into practice every day. Brian Robertson, founder of the management style holacracy, sent me an unpublished final chapter for his book by the same name. The book's editors weren't ready for such subversive thinking, so they rejected that chapter. But we're ready. With Robertson's permission in hand, I'm going to quote extensively:

> Perhaps this then is the next step for our current societal governance. Perhaps it's time to allow the centralized power of current governments to give way and dissolve, and allow new methods of achieving order to emerge from

the ashes—ones that don't have legislators and regulators to buy, or the power to make aggression legal or peaceful exchange illegal. Ones that are themselves subject to the forces of evolution and selection based on the value they add, rather than holding themselves outside of that process as monopoly providers. When I share this view of a possible next-step for society, I sometimes get confused questions of why I'm advocating anarchy—especially when the main focus of my work is all about governance systems and authority structures.

Oh my. Did Robertson just use the A-word?

I think this usually comes from people who think of anarchy as a system without rules or order, and assume a system without top-down government must also lack rules and order. Yet if we look at the etymology of the word "anarchy", a different connotation takes shape, and one that actually fits both Holacracy and the vision I'm offering here quite well. Anarchy comes from the greek "an", meaning without, plus "arkhos", meaning rulers. Anarchy doesn't mean without rules, but without rulers. If you have the right rules, the absence of top-down rulers doesn't remove order —it simply enables order to emerge dynamically from peer-to-peer interactions distributed throughout a system, one tension at a time. So by this definition, you could describe Holacracy as a rule system for humans working together in anarchy—with rules, but without rulers.

The incentives for social change are already strong—so strong that the gales of creative destruction can finally demolish much of the state apparatus, which seemed impervious to reform. And that's a good thing for a self-governing people.

The celebrated historian Frederick Jackson Turner summed up his famous treatise on the American West agreeing—perhaps despite himself—that people of the frontier had been moving away from command and control.

"In spite of environment, and in spite of custom," wrote Turner in his famous essay, "each frontier did indeed furnish a new field of opportunity, a gate of escape from the bondage of the past; and freshness, and confidence, and scorn of older society, impatience of its restraints and its ideas, and indifference to its lessons, have accompanied the frontier."[175]

But in 1893, as Turner penned that passage, the frontier had already closed.

Nowadays, seekers and strivers have reopened the frontier, no longer a peculiarly American terrain. It's a space beyond nation or territory—without end and without the need for Caesar's imprimatur. As people start to gather there, there will be every form of vice, as in the past. But there will also be rapid advances and innovative wonders. Everything will be subject to continual trial, error, and revision. And paradoxically, that infinite space in which we can spread out and try new things enables us to be closer than ever before.

Venture fund manager Michael P. Gibson thinks the nation-state era is coming to a close.

"For over 350 years Westphalian sovereignty has rooted its authority and expressed its power along territorial borders, lines demarcating a state's monopoly on the legitimate use of violence. Space and time are its key coordinates. Any x and y for longitude and latitude determine which laws apply."[176]

Up to this point, roving conquerors put flags in soil. As long as they could hold the territory and keep the people submissive, the conquerors' rules were everyone's. "Citizens have by and large remained stationary," Gibson explains, "hemmed in or locked out, albeit with some in and out flow. But over time those in power have changed. Government actors vary after some duration, either by coup, by annexation, by succession of the throne, or by—the current best case—the preferences of voters in elections."

But the age of exit is upon us.

"We are entering an era when governance and citizenship will decouple from location," thinks Gibson. "And because of that, the purveyors of bad laws will fade away and good laws will surface to dominate the law market in the century ahead."[177]

Under systems of competitive governance, ideology takes a back seat to real human choices. If you think you've got a better system, you'll have to build it. The days of building utopias through power and violence are going away, because governance will function more like a service in a market. Indeed, if there is real competition among systems of governance, there is less likely to be unsustainable corruption. After all, corruption is just the sort of human phenomenon that drives people—i.e. governance customers—away.

Some readers will not be comfortable with the idea that governance will soon be the product of innovation and competition. Almost daily we read pleas to "fix democracy" or to adopt some sophisticated technical kludge like liquid democracy. But that's just trying to rescue voice and loyalty in an onrushing age of exit.

We're becoming cultural cosmopolitans, radical communitarians, and standard bearers for a right of exit. Most importantly, we're freer than ever before. In the infinite realms of the cloud, there will be less room for politicians with big plans. They'll find it difficult to impose hierarchy on the new frontier folk who will run among network nodes.

CHAPTER SEVEN

VALUES
FOR A POST-POLITICAL AGE

My position is not incompatible with urging that we try to extend our sense of "we" to people whom we have previously thought of as "they."

— Richard Rorty[178]

PSILOCYBIN IS A POWERFUL COMPOUND found in a fungus. Whether you think of it as a hippie drug or a shortcut to satori, there's no doubt that it can be life changing.

After one takes magic mushrooms, one can usually check off William James's four dimensions of mystical experience: the experience is nearly impossible to put into words (ineffability); though inarticulable, it confers knowledge (noetic quality); it comes and goes (transiency); and it cannot be initiated, but must be revealed (passivity).

One experiences the fractal aesthetics of a brain making new connections. In some cases, the subject experiences the dissolution of ego or the stretching of time. The categories "I" and "we" aren't so fixed anymore, either, as one comes to regard other perspectives as being portals into a greater All-mind. Once the peak has passed, one is left with a residue of insight and a feeling of increased well-being. If nothing else, what one usually *can* articulate about a psychedelic experience is that one feels a profound sense of connection to everything and everyone.

Even the most cynical atheists have come away describing the experience as spiritual. Still, a rational materialist might explain such experiences as simply the loss of contact with reality, that is, the consequence of eating something that futzes with normal brain chemistry. To mystics, entheogens are a means to accessing a spiritual universe that is far more vast and meaningful than what the materialist mind can fully apprehend.

Can we stake out a sweet spot between these two poles? The future might depend on it.

In 2008, neuroscientist Roland Griffiths and his team tested psilocybin on thirty-six "hallucinogen-naïve" humans. The result was:

> At the 14-month follow-up, 58% and 67%, respectively, of volunteers rated the psilocybin-occasioned experience as being among *the five most personally meaningful* and among *the five most spiritually significant experiences of their lives*; 64% indicated the experience increased well-being or life satisfaction; 58% met criteria for having had a "complete" mystical experience.[179]

The preceding results are promising for many reasons, but in every such "complete mystical experience" there is surely the knowledge that we all are somehow connected, or at least that we should be.

If William James's criteria are correct, translating mystical insights into a rationalist's lexicon rather misses the point. Or as Louis Armstrong said when asked to describe jazz: "Man, if you have to ask what it is, you'll never know." But we have to take a risk with that clumsy symbol system we call language. Our goal, after all, is to point to a new set of postpolitical values.

Those who have not taken an entheogen or had a complete mystical experience will probably regard this discussion with skepticism, even cynicism. What could our hippie friends possibly have to teach us about feeling more "connected" with humanity? And what could possibly be useful about these peak experiences otherwise?

Psychedelics have the potential quite literally to change one's personality. In fact, people not only report something like, "it opened my mind," but that the mind opening persists. In a number of studies, psychologists have used the Big

Five personality battery to test these reports. Using substances, such as LSD and psilocybin, people can move higher on this dimension for weeks or even months.

Becoming more open minded is one thing. But these substances have just as profound an effect on our moral psychology, particularly when it comes to authority.

In the journal *Psychopharmacology*, Taylor Lyons and Robin Carhart-Harris report on a pilot study showing that "psilocybin with psychological support might produce lasting changes in attitudes and beliefs." Specifically, they conclude that nature relatedness increased and authoritarianism decreased in subjects, even after many months.[180]

Administered in responsible therapeutic settings, entheogens could be a path to reckoning with the profound changes ahead. Indeed, when we realize that personality is one of the strongest determinants of cultural values, we might conclude that psychedelics could be yet another technology for the coming era— whether in preparing for or catalyzing it. We needn't belabor this idea, though. The point is that it will be important to open our minds, consider new perspectives, and embrace new values even if it means going against the grain. Cognitive and cultural flexibility will be necessary for adapting to the fluid circumstances of the social singularity.

Some readers might be horrified by the idea of using psychedelics for personality augmentation. Most Americans have a collective picture of bacchanalian hippies, dancing in the mud, losing their grip on reality. Or, we can imagine dystopian scenarios in which authoritarians introduce mass treatment regimes to make the rest of the population more pliant. My suggestion here is far more modest: The liberalization of psychedelics could offer a tool for those who wish to open their minds or have spiritual experience. A happy side effect might be that those who choose to use psychedelic technologies are better prepared for the coming age.

What Rational Mysticism Has to Teach Us

In 1962, "I, Pencil" author Leonard Read wrote that one "who acknowledges an infinite consciousness cannot help respecting fellow human beings as the apertures through whom infinite consciousness flows and manifests itself."[181]

Notice he did not say "higher power." He could just as well have been writing as a Buddhist would have in that passage. While Read believed in God, the evocation of an infinite consciousness of which we are all part is not your run-of-the-mill God talk, especially not in America circa 1962.

For Read, it is a way of reconciling individualism with a deep regard for others, who are, to him, sacred aspects of a larger self or interconnected set of selves. This variation on the golden rule may strike us as rather strange, for it is both individualistic and collectivistic (or maybe it's neither). Read's view represents in some sense an integration of self and others that offers a different kind of entry point for a movement. In this way, Read was anticipating the kind of mindset needed for radical decentralization as we approach the social singularity. Much like the ancients in India who spoke of *ahimsa*, which means "compassion" or "not to injure," Read was committed to a doctrine of anything peaceful, and this virtue of nonviolence seems to be a residue both of meditation and of mushrooms.

Fast-forward to the twenty-first century. In anticipating the era of connection and complexity, we are searching for the right values, the right balance of "we" and "I."

"In this post-collectivist future, the individual won't be either supreme or irrelevant," writes software developer Justin Goro. "Instead, choices of individuals will be so strongly influenced by programmable incentives that distinctions between individual welfare and the greater good will lose meaning."[182]

So our old rules are holding us back. In today's politics, groups of individuals "gather together and exploit other groups for differential gain," adds Goro. "The net effect of such action always undermines the overall wealth of society."[183] That's politics. Such a condition gives rise to unhealthy behaviors. But as we approach the social singularity, we are approaching a different way of organizing ourselves—a latticework of win-win-win relationships, accompanied by a different set of cultural values that work in the service of forming and keeping those relationships.

From those who write software, this kind of anti-establishment language might elicit sneers. After all, code is based in logic. And logic's philosophical tradition has origins in the Enlightenment. Software developers are people of reason who appreciate evidence.

But we needn't give up our reason to embrace the mystical. It is rather a mode of experience or understanding we may not be used to. Such may be difficult to articulate in the language of Western rationalism, but experience of ineffable knowledge often points to what is possible, even if only in glimpses. A sense of connection lays the groundwork for a value system that impels us more quickly toward the social singularity, just as the technology of the social singularity impels us towards a sense of connection, towards ahimsa.

Ecstasis, "I," and "We"

When we think of mystics, it's easy to think of something like shamanic primitivism—that is, of pagans in robes spinning myths about the heavens, or simple peoples ascribing spirits to rocks and sticks. While there is something about this stereotype that offends our Western sensibilities, we also have much to learn from these traditions—particularly in their experience of *ecstasis*.

"The Eleusinian Mysteries," write Jamie Wheal and Steven Kotler in *Stealing Fire*, "were an elaborate nine-day ritual designed to strip away standard frames of reference, profoundly alter consciousness, and unlock a heightened level of insight."

Ancient Greek Burning Man, perhaps.

"Specifically, the mysteries combined a number of state-changing techniques— fasting, singing, dancing, drumming, costumes, dramatic storytelling, physical exhaustion, and *kykeon* . . . to induce a cathartic experience of death, rebirth, and 'divine inspiration.'"[184]

We have much to learn and reintegrate from these traditions, explain Wheal and Kotler, especially as there is power in the experience of the contingent self and the connected self.

> During ecstasis, our sense of being an individual "I" gets replaced by the feeling of being a collective "we." And this doesn't just happen in small groups like the [US Navy] SEALS on night ops or Googlers at a desert festival. It's also the feeling that arises at large political rallies, rock concerts, and sporting events. . . . Bring a large group of people together, deploy a suite of mind-melding technolo-

gies, and suddenly everyone's consciousness is doing the
wave.[185]

As we approach the social singularity we will become more cognizant of our
human interdependence. And that interdependence will cause us to regard one
another not just as strangers operating in a market, but also as empathic entities
who compose a holistic set of systems and subsystems that is greater than the
sum of its parts.

Beyond Individualism and Collectivism

In their influential book, *Spiral Dynamics*, social psychologists Don Edward
Beck and Christopher C. Cowan describe phases of human development over
the ages. The phase Beck and Cowan believe is the most recent in human history and is still developing, they label Turquoise. The Turquoise level is an in-
tegrative system that "combines an organism's necessary self-interest with the
interests of the communities in which it participates."[186]

This way of seeing the world is neither rugged individualism nor crude commu-
nitarianism. It requires seeing ourselves through others and others through ourselves. Of course, politics obstructs this way of seeing, whether we want it to or
not.

Can we believe not only that each of us is sacred as a distinct self, but also that
we are all connected and are becoming more and more connected each day?
Could it be that each of us—each self—is a window, an "aperture" into a
greater consciousness to which we all belong? And even if such beliefs were
only metaphorically true, would not the adoption of those beliefs improve the
lot of humanity? Our ability to make this perspectival shift will empower us to
manage humanity's great becoming.

Maybe a superconsciousness will emerge in the future, a future in which we are
now participating with every choice we make. The connections we form may
be as mundane as a single transaction, a nod to a neighbor, or a "like" on social
media. But the totality of our connections can give rise to something as complex as the Internet, or something as *infinitely* complex as a set of human minds
networked in some post-singularity world.

One major breakthrough in our social evolution—in moving beyond territory
and tribe—was passing into a commercial condition. The current stage, build-

ing on that condition, is radical connectivity. What will the next stage be? A confluence of minds? The rational mystic holds out for the possibility that our peaceful interactions—drawing us together as they do—could accumulate layer by layer, culminating in a future that would make us weep if we could see it. That future might well be functional, rational, and orderly. But just to imagine it right now is to appreciate the ongoing, imperfect unfolding of change within ourselves and our world. To imagine it now, we have to make a bit of room for the mystical and suspend our disbelief a little about technology facilitating a kind of magic, at least in the spirit of Clarke's Third Law.[187]

Values Reframed

To spend time with subversive innovators, it would seem the social singularity will be driven primarily by technological innovation. In other words, technology is a leading indicator of societal change—and this is likely to be truer than ever in the coming decades. Politics, though still potent, will slowly lose its central place in human affairs. Innovation will usurp politics.

And thank the gods.

None of this means that cultural values are but a lagging indicator or some inert epiphenomenon. Yes, we shape our tools and our tools shape us. We shape our rules and our rules shape us. But it is just as vital to understand that *we shape our values and our values shape us*. After all, there is nothing value-free about writing a line of code or inventing an alternative energy source.

In other words, cultural values will both drive and be a byproduct of the movement toward the social singularity. In a couple of respects, writing these very words is a way to create a self-fulfilling prophecy. This is a cultural product with an embedded set of values. I freely admit that *The Social Singularity* is both a positive and a normative work. It's about how human society *is* developing, as well as how it *ought* to. And this book is just one example of how we can avoid the naturalistic fallacy and still create works that touch on important questions of both *is* and *ought* without lapsing into contradiction.

We can start by reframing our thinking—from a political frame to an innovative frame. As a cultural disposition, that means our first instinct should be neither to bring all of our grievances to the streets, nor to drop them into a political sausage grinder. Instead, we can take our problems to the laboratory, as it were, and "criticize by creating." We can start experimenting with programmable incentives and novel ways of organizing ourselves so as to attract new members to new communities of practice. Within those communities, new values will emerge, and those values that both *create* and *are a product of* aligned incentives are likely to survive the evolutionary gauntlet.

Ascending the Spiral

Since Don Beck and Christopher Cowan published *Spiral Dynamics*—popularizing the work of psychologist Clare Graves—practitioners, from management gurus to statesmen, have used the book's framework to change companies, lead nations, or simply understand the peoples of the world. The theory is now mature. Beck has applied it in a number of important contexts, such as helping Nelson Mandela craft a post-apartheid peace in South Africa.

Critics have argued that Spiral Dynamics is in certain respects too vague and in other respects too reductionist. For our purposes, though, it is at least a useful heuristic. As the world becomes more complex, we need to adopt values that enable us to live in a condition of greater complexity.

In case you're not familiar with Spiral Dynamics, let's do a little review.

The Spiral Dynamics framework postulates that people, both as individuals and as groups, pass through psychosocial stages of development. Each stage, known as a *v-meme* (for "value meme"), includes a set of associated values, which Beck and Cowan believe help people to function and sometimes thrive in different life circumstances. The stages are rooted in evolutionary biology and have emerged along with our development as a species. In other respects, the stages unfold with our development as social creatures living in certain environments throughout history. No need to rehash the nature-nurture debates here, as both are important to Spiral Dynamics.

As we change our circumstances and develop new systems of living together, we improve our cognitive states and change our values, too. These values tend to cluster, as we'll see. The totality is represented by an upward-flowing spiral, which each of us as full human beings can ascend.

Each stage of development in Spiral Dynamics is represented by a color. As individuals (or sometimes a whole population) ascend the spiral, they pass through various v-memes and adopt the values associated with that stage. A number of psychologists and social theorists have proposed similar developmental models. But Spiral Dynamics is among the most robust in that it is one of the easiest to apply within different social contexts.

The Spiral: First Tier

We begin with Beige. In this first stage of the spiral, the values are simple survival. Food, water, shelter, and sleep. In this stage, people live pretty much on instincts alone. But soon we bond with others, usually kin.

From Beige, we move into Purple. In this stage lie the values of the tribe or clan. Here we find rudimentary kinship ties, ancestor worship, and a preoccupation with magic, blessings, curses, and juju (mysticism). Indeed, in a world of scarce resources and unforgiving nature, there is strength in one's family group.

But when clans collide and compete for resources, another cluster of values, or v-meme, emerges. So after Purple comes Red. Values in this stage include a desire for power, glory, and conquest. The basic value system requires us to recognize threats around us and to prevail at all costs. Otherwise, enjoy yourself to the fullest and with no regrets—for tomorrow you could be dead. When the world around you is violent, you battle till you die or stand, bloody, clutching the treasures of the vanquished.

After conquest is complete and enemies brought to heel, we must all become more civilized. The values of Blue mute the excesses of Red and include loyalty, order, and deference to the plans of higher authority. We achieve order through understanding our place in a great hierarchy. And a Blue order requires adherence to strict rules of right and wrong.

But Blue can be stiff and suffocating. The intellectually curious, through experimentation and observation, find their way to science. The ambitious, oriented to success, find their way to commerce. These are the values of Orange, which work in a world of natural laws and no-nonsense economics.

But have we lost our sensitivity? Our community? The earth? Green asks us to consider an ethic of care and a politics of equality. We should be sharing more, and in decisions we should be seeking democratic consensus. Everyone has a voice, and each voice is equally valid (as long as that voice speaks Green's v-memes).

Such is the first tier of Spiral Dynamics. Depending on the context in which a person finds herself, each of these sets of values is justifiable. While such a claim might invite theoretical or even moral objections, suffice it to say that these values have enabled people to survive and thrive throughout history. In this way, though we might not say that the values of each color track with some universal or Platonic good, v-memes have helped people to get through their circumstances and move on to new circumstances, which require embracing new values.

Currently, the second tier stages await most of humanity. But for us to move en masse into the second tier requires a leap where, according to Clare Graves, "a chasm of unbelievable depth of meaning is crossed."[188]

The Spiral: Second Tier

Before we get into the second tier, consider that as we move up the spiral we pass through "we"-centered v-memes (as represented by the cool colors purple, blue, and green), and through "I"-centered v-memes (as represented by the warm colors beige, red, and orange). This moving back and forth between "I"- and "we"-centered value systems is a natural part of the process when ascending the spiral.

Now, just when we thought we had found our humanity in Green, we realized that all the feel-good relativism, faux toleration, and postmodern claptrap has made us feel cut adrift at best; dogmatic, violent, and intolerant at worst. We must make the jump to Yellow—the first stage of the second tier.

In Yellow we find first that we have transcended all those prior value systems, but we find also that we can look back to each stage and appreciate the value in it as necessity dictates. We can do so without judgment because we are flexible, adaptive systems thinkers. We know we are interdependent beings, and yet we require some degree of autonomy and respect equal autonomy in others.

Diverse people with diverse values can be integrated with flexible rules and protocols. And we understand that from relative autonomy, complexity emerges. Organic "growth" hierarchies are tolerated, as Yellow leaders find they can see much more of the spiral in those around them.

Swinging from Yellow to Turquoise is a smaller jump. Instead of responding to the prior stage with hostility, we embrace and transcend the flexibility, autonomy and systems thinking of Yellow, but also begin to expand our perspective to include the fluid, dynamic relationships between parts and wholes, wholes and parts. We understand ourselves within the context of a wider ecosystem that is the world, and we know that our small behaviors can ripple to big effects —for good and ill. Turquoise can detect harmonies and disharmonies in multiple, nested spheres of interaction at multiple levels of description.

Spirituality under this view is not mere myth and mysticism, but an internalized understanding of all life as an interconnected meshwork. Perhaps you can start to see how Yellow and Turquoise could be the value stages that act as handmaiden to the social singularity.

Values of the Coming Era

Earlier in this book, we considered the guardian and commercial syndromes Jacobs described and the honor, dignity, and victim cultures identified by Campbell and Manning. It's no accident that both of these analyses of human values track, at least roughly, with Spiral Dynamics v-memes. Honor culture, for example, has many of the features of Blue, dignity culture of Orange, and victim culture of Green.

Recognizing patterns of cultural values at this level of description can help us to deal with changes in contemporary life—and thrive in them. The tendency of certain values to coevolve as survival systems has interesting implications: most human beings have the potential for all syndromes, though to varying degrees. From the standpoint of evolutionary psychology, we're still cave people.

Rather than recreating the nature-nurture debates here, let's suppose we're all still saddled with a host of moral dispositions that enabled us to get along out on the steppe. In some people, Purple (or we might call it "clan syndrome") is going to be stronger—to *feel* stronger. In others, guardian syndrome will predominate, and still others will exhibit traits of commercial syndrome far more readily. Of course, as syndromes overlap, we might get even more interesting and contradictory as a moral species. We will have to develop metavalues.

We are not fully controlled by our genetic programming. As stated, at the level of the group, moral syndromes probably coevolve with survival (incentive) systems, as people will often revise their commitments in the face of strong incentives. The instincts are still there, but perhaps buried. And, indeed, many of us will suppress competing syndrome traits as we are impressed from time to time by rhetoric or rational argument from masters of moral language.

Social psychologist Jonathan Haidt reminds us:

> If you think that moral reasoning is something we do to fig-
> ure out the truth, you'll be constantly frustrated by how
> foolish, biased, and illogical people become when they dis-
> agree with you. But if you think about moral reasoning as a
> skill we humans evolved to further our social agendas—to
> justify our own actions and to defend the teams we belong
> to—then things will make a lot more sense. Keep your eye
> on the intuitions, and don't take people's moral arguments
> at face value. They're mostly post hoc constructions made
> up on the fly, crafted to advance one or more strategic ob-
> jectives.[189]

In all of our political wrangling, moralizing, and wars, commitments within multiple syndromes operating all at once mean that humanity undergoes no seamless phase transitions. Ideas become complex intellectual latticeworks around these evolving dispositions and their accompanying values. In some sense, this is the power of ideology: ideas and our very human dispositions operate in close tandem. And that's one reason why people fight for ideology—in jungles, in politics, or on college campuses. Syndromes can awaken and reawaken in us. And phase transitions proceed in fits and starts.

But they do proceed. And as these transitions reshape the incentive structures of humanity, our moral universes get reshaped, too. And, of course, moral universes can affect the incentive structures. Each force pulls the other along. This coevolution of institutions and moral syndromes should make us pause a bit before accepting notions of transcendent virtues, moral foundations, or universalistic theories of justice. Without rekindling debates about the relationship between institutions and ideas, or debates about the existence of moral absolutes, I instead suggest that taking a systems view of morality and human progress can lead us to appreciate what lies ahead.

A New Syndrome

With a new structural reality emerging, a new syndrome is likely to emerge. This largely transpartisan, postpolitical state of affairs will not be some techno-utopia. It will come with its own set of problems. Human history, however, despite fits and starts, will at the very least restore the phrase "all politics is local." People increasingly will exercise voice within tighter communities of practice to convince members to go along with their ways of seeing things or join their network tribe. But as we build a great, conceptual open-source layer spanning the globe, the mores of a new syndrome will come to dominate our behavior both online and in meatspace.

We already can see shoots of this new cluster sprouting in the frantic and hopeful emergence of the tokenized economy. Call it "connection syndrome." At its best, it will look something like:

1. Be visionary.
2. See beyond politics as a means of change.
3. Be experimental and generative.
4. Share abundance liberally and intelligently.
5. Be open, adaptive, and tolerant of diversity.
6. Seek to integrate.
7. Form and join communities of agreement.
8. Exit communities that aren't working.
9. Change the world by creating new options.
10. Accept that ideas are gifts to the commons.
11. Tolerate inequality, but create abundance.
12. Welcome interdependence.
13. Cultivate trust systems and networks.
14. Reconnect with nature.
15. Be more cosmopolitan.
16. Work to build something greater than oneself while understanding how one fits in.
17. Leave formal hierarchies behind; enter networks and growth hierarchies.
18. Promote experience and meaning over material things.
19. Consider how parts and wholes interrelate.
20. Cultivate wonder, rather than fear, in the face of change.
21. Hold reverence for nonlinear systems.
22. Look for how things flow; ask how they can flow better.
23. Look inward, not just outward, for change.
24. Take the "meta" view now and again.

Relative to the population, only a few at first will embrace this cluster of values. Those holding these values will be pioneers of the ideas set out here. Visualize people's progress through clusters of values on a bell curve. The bulge of the bell curve is currently straddling Orange and Green value systems in most Western countries, with a shrinking Blue population on the trailing tail of the curve and a tiny population of Yellow (and a miniscule one of Turquoise) at the leading tail.

Connection syndrome is our big cluster concept, then, for people who are comfortable with subversive innovation. We are the standard bearers for a future in which a better world can be dreamed by visionaries, socially constructed, and hard-coded into existence. As dreamers and doers, we are prepared to forgo the spectacle of elections and the blood sport of campaign politics. We want to take a vantage point from high above, looking at how we can reweave the lattice-work of human interaction to create a great reconciliation between private interest and community good. We want to set about our quests as twenty-first century pioneers armed with a reflective, conscientious mien and the knowledge that we can operate as a human hive mind to create a world of beauty and wonder. Our children will enter that world seamlessly, growing up as self-actualized learners with eyes wide open as the social singularity binds us in new forms of collective consciousness.

Connection syndrome is meant to more-or-less align with the Yellow (systems) and to some extent Turquoise (holism) stages of Spiral Dynamics. To die-hard practitioners, this combining probably is considered heresy, as one cannot simply blend v-memes willy-nilly. My purpose here is to point the way. Those interested in parsing the details should look into matters further. That said, it is crucial to take a moment to talk about where we've come from.

On Prior Values

One of Spiral Dynamics' best-known practitioners is controversial theoretician Ken Wilber, who reminds us that any new stage or syndrome "embraces and transcends" prior stages and syndromes. "That is, each wave goes beyond (or transcends) its predecessor, and yet it includes or embraces it in its own makeup. For example, a cell transcends but includes molecules, which transcend but include atoms."[190]

In this way, prior stages are fundamental to all subsequent stages. Prior stages should not be rejected or marginalized. Sadly, it appears that many who have ascended the spiral to the second tier (or entered connection syndrome) have lost the ability consciously to transcend and include. For if nothing else, contemporary politics demonstrates a struggle among first-tier stages, with each stage lacking any real understanding of the other. Prior stages simply don't understand stages above them because they have not yet ascended. And stages above them have forgotten where they came from and how prior stages fit.

To cross the chasm from first to second tier is to, in Wilber's words, "for the first time, *vividly grasp the entire spectrum of interior development,* and thus see that each level, each meme, each wave is crucially important for the health of the overall Spiral."[191]

Thus, we can do better—right here, right now. At the very least, hurtling towards the social singularity requires us to leap the chasm. Some will not be ready. An intrepid group of us must be willing to ascend consciously.

Unhealthy Expressions

Currently, the dominant value systems, or v-memes, in the US are Blue, Orange, and Green. Conservatives are typically at the Blue level, while liberals are generally at the Green; there's considerable overlap in Orange. Each of these first-tier stages has healthy and unhealthy expressions. In contemporary American politics, though, they seem to express their unhealthiest aspects. Perhaps these unhealthy expressions have been most acutely revealed during the campaign, election, and presidency of Donald Trump.

"The leading-edge of cultural evolution is today—and has been for four or five decades—the green wave,"[192] writes Wilber, who opines that the reaction to Donald Trump's election has been a manifestation of "Mean Green Meme." Likewise, Trump's election had been a reaction to Green's excesses, including hyper-egalitarianism, identity politics, and a perpetual-victim culture that could awaken outrage at the smallest perceived slight. Mobs of righteous crusaders have ended careers based on unproven accusations or ideological differences—perhaps due to something said in poor taste or the appearance of impropriety.

Students and professors have shut down speech and debate on campuses, branding any idea outside of Green's orthodoxy as evil, racist, sexist, or all of the above. Any "rights of the accused" were meaningless vestiges of Orange. The ends of social justice justified the means. What might have started as shaming practices quickly escalated into protests that ended in property damage and violence.

The response to Green's unhealthy convulsions? Crude Blue withdrew into nativism and intolerance. Rotten Orange revealed a get-mine capitalism and an insensitivity to everything it perceived as politically correct. Blue and Orange went so far out of their way to be un-PC that many would live in denial about victims of police abuse or sexual assault. Some would even don the mantle of the alt-right, at first to razz Mean Greens, but perhaps later to swallow their own poisonous doctrines. The result has been not a healthy or coherent set of values but a mess that, as of this writing, we're still experiencing.

Healthy Expressions

"The worst in our nature coexists with the best," states the great biologist E. O. Wilson, "and so it will ever be."[193] The question before us, then, is: How can we encourage our fellows to return to the healthier values of their stages or syndromes? How can we help others to "level up," where appropriate, that is, to ascend the spiral of psychosocial development to discover the best aspects of themselves?

The answer to such questions would, I gather, require an entire volume. Maybe it's enough here to act as an old, wise man along the path, pointing the way to values that, hopefully, can restrain our lesser angels.

At the very least, people at the second tier can show the way in their actions. In some practical sense, that means we can respectfully see when to adopt the mores needed to thrive wherever we are. We can thus wear the Red jersey when coaching a kids' ball game, don that Blue suit when visiting the grandparents at their church, pull out the strategic Orange power tie at a business lunch, or brandish our Green credentials at a community cleanup meeting.

Being a healthy Yellow doesn't mean we must always act as chameleons, though. In some contexts, we have to learn when to enculturate healthy values that enable others to level up, though that requires what Beck and Cowan call "Spiral Wizardry." A spiral wizard knows how to assist with ascent. A healthy Blue can help a Red to appreciate law and order. A healthy Orange can help a Blue to question unexamined assumptions about authority. A healthy Green can help an Orange to be a more conscientious capitalist. And a healthy Yellow can help a Green to recognize the folly of simplistic egalitarianism. Beck and Cowan continue:

"Spiral Wizards rely on two guiding principles. First, they seek to *assist each v-meme to develop* Horizontally and remain in a healthy condition so that it can add to the life of the Spiral. Second, they strive to *keep the Spiral open* Vertically so new v-memes can awaken and Obliquely so the existing ones can adjust as *Life Conditions* dictate."[194]

In this great nexus of interlocking values, there is room for growth. And that growth often starts when one looks inward.

The Value of Exploring One's Inner Life

Much of our effort has been dedicated to discussing the function and form of society's evolution as we approach the social singularity. But that doesn't mean we should be preoccupied with the external. If we can learn anything from Eastern traditions, it's that we have much to explore within ourselves.

It's no accident that people are learning to meditate, to practice mindfulness, and to be grateful for the simplest things. Learning to manage stress and civilization's constant mental and media chatter is a necessary reaction to living in an increasingly complex world. But stress management can also be a gateway drug to a richer inner life.

The practices of inner exploration not only offer the benefits of improved well-being, but complement the values of connection syndrome and second-tier v-memes. As we discussed in the section above titled "Rediscovering Our Humanity," we have an unprecedented opportunity to reacquaint ourselves with the true, the beautiful, and the good. But part of that reacquaintance starts with reconditioning our inner lives to explore and accept these timeless gifts.

Going deeper, a psychonaut can learn spiritual resilience, developing a more detached and circumspect view that accompanies a maturing affect. And most importantly, an inner explorer could arrive at peak experiences without the aid of pharmaceuticals. Along the way, the discipline and practice of tending to one's inner life has myriad associated benefits, which include adopting a beginner's mind. [195]

A Beginner's Mind

One day, my son Sid and I were looking at various rocks in his collection. He was about six at the time. I used to get frustrated at that bucket of rocks. He'd put any old rock in there, and he found a new one practically every day. The collection got heavy.

"We have rocks coming out of our ears," I said. So I asked him about his collection, pointing out certain rocks to see why he liked them. Each time, he would find some little detail—a color, a glint.

"You might not think this one is that great," he said, picking up a plain one, "but look at that peach color." It really did have a beauty if you looked closely enough.

"All right," I replied. "But what about this one? It's boring."

"Oh," he said, "you're looking the wrong way, Dad. Don't use your eyes."

He put it into my hand. It was the smoothest stone I'd touched.

Starting Points

My son had taught me something important that day. His fresh look at the world prompted me to shed certain assumptions. As it is with rocks, so it is with people.

For most people, emotional value centers are inborn. A mentor, a book, or a life event activates these centers, and they start to build an intellectual latticework around them. "Like everyone else, philosophers measure their personal emotional responses to various alternatives as though consulting a hidden oracle," E. O. Wilson writes in *On Human Nature*.

> That oracle resides in the deep emotional centers of the brain, most probably with the limbic system, a complex array of neurons and hormone-secreting cells located just beneath the "thinking" portion of the cerebral cortex. Human emotional responses and the more general ethical practices based on them have been programmed to a substantial degree by natural selection over thousands of generations.[196]

How's that for an axiom?

Here's where things get crucial: some subversive innovators want people to have more agency. Other subversive innovators want to help the most vulnerable in society. These moral sentiments are evolved starting points, and each is important. But recognizing different starting points means it's time to expand our conception of cultural values. Your moral frame or mine works great when we speak the same moral language. But we must first acknowledge that morality is a Tower of Babel. In fact, if you believe Jonathan Haidt in *The Righteous Mind*, it can be quite rare to find full consensus. Different moral starting points are endemic.

"Morality binds and blinds," writes Haidt. "It binds us into ideological teams that fight each other as though the fate of the world depended on our side winning each battle. It blinds us to the fact that each team is composed of good people who have something important to say."[197]

It doesn't matter if you think that people have inalienable natural rights, or that the consequences of one body of rules or another will be positive, or that the classical virtues provide the best guidance. What matters is that those who are listening will come into any contact with you carrying certain ideological baggage. They will be disposed differently. To bring them around to your way of seeing things is *first* to understand them and to empathize with them—at least in some measure. It requires pulling them into solidarity with you by helping them to reweave their web of beliefs, all with a willingness to reweave your own.

Holists and Solipsists

Holists are fluent in multiple moral languages. It's not easy. Even the most accomplished people might not be fluent in more than one. It doesn't matter how smart some economics professor is, for example. The breadth and depth of her thinking may be constrained either by her specialization or by some utilitarian starting points. A man may be an accomplished scribe in a long tradition of scribes but have only a rudimentary grasp of concepts like virtue, duty, and rhetoric. Likewise, a philosopher may make great syllogisms but not have the gift of gab, exude charm, or shake the brightest tail feathers. Yet it is often these compelling traits that can pull an intellectually curious person into a new community's orbit.

True holists are rare today, but they will be increasingly vital as we enter the postpolitical era.

At the other end of the continuum from the holist is the solipsist. This person is content in the echo chamber, sometimes being alone with his principles. Solipsists can be valuable stalwarts for solidarity, because even though they operate in an echo chamber, they can help to hold it together. Healthy solipsists will remind you in a reasonable way when you might be straying too far off the reservation. And they are good at finding other solipsists who share their particular starting points. But an unhealthy solipsist is strident, rabid, axiom-obsessed, dogmatic, or linear. Many are enamored at the idea of being in an exclusive club, rejecting those whom they see as apostate.

More of us should either aspire to be holists, or at least respect those who are going about skinning life's cat in different ways. Because after a certain point, solipsism is only good for indulging some urge to get attention. Anyone who wants to build a broader community—that is, to persuade a critical mass of human souls—has to be prepared to diversify, to think across multiple perspectives, and to understand the values of those who start at different points. Those who can do all that will rise to soaring heights.

Two Forces of Change

It takes a lot more effort to have a conversation across great ideological gulfs than to fire missiles across them. But we must make the effort. Because there are certain, though perhaps unsettling, human truths we all have to face.

First, there are only two forces of societal change in this world that matter: persuasion and coercion. One can hold all the principles and axioms he likes, but the people with the jails, the guns, and the jackboots may not care about those principles.

Second, those committed to peaceful means of social change have only persuasion at their disposal. So if we think that using violence is wrong, we'd better become master persuaders—effective holists—willing to stare through others' lenses and find a way to connect with their values before those with guns, jails, and jackboots do. The social singularity is not, after all, a foregone conclusion. Powerful authoritarians are waiting to cast us into another Dark Age. Indeed, the closer we get to the social singularity, the more authoritarians—and the beneficiaries of the status quo they protect—will feel threatened by change.

Given the foregoing, solipsists may accuse me of being a moral relativist. Those who do will be missing the point. Subversive innovators are effective only to the degree that we can grow our ranks, lock arms, and build a freer world as the power hierarchies of the twentieth century crumble. Being a holist is about searching for all the reasons people ought to share our new syndrome and celebrating the areas of overlap. We will never fully agree about everything, but we will be more united in our diversity.

This complete, multifaceted movement will one day be more powerful than any coercive government, because the people who make it up will be able to open others' eyes to subtler colors and smoother surfaces. Beneath it all, we will discover what we have in common—our connection, our humanity, and our capacity for love.

A PROMISING
AND TROUBLING POSSIBILITY

Behold the entire cosmos turning
within my body, and the other
things you desire to see.
— The Bhagavad Gita[198]

A HUMAN BRAIN is delicate. It's about three pounds and gray on the outside, with a consistency of firm pudding or Jell-O. That jelly holds a mesh of billions of neurons, which transmit information in fractions of a second. Each of us needs this complex structure because it is responsible for everything we do. We use it to understand the world, to think, to feel, to live in the world, and to dream of worlds beyond. Our brain represents *our* reality and negotiates how we function within it.

Currently, our brain is the most complex machine in existence, and yet we really don't fully get how it works. We have clues. We find patterns. We analyze the brain at different levels of description with biology, chemistry, and medicine. Though we can divide the brain into modules with certain functionality, we're still unable to explain how it coordinates activities and develops language, intentionality, consciousness, and a sense of self. These mental aspects are closely connected to, but distinct from, the brain. When we speak of mental properties, we're referring to aspects of our thoughts and experiences. When we talk about our brains, we're referring to physical things that have certain functions that give rise to our minds.

But as we come to understand our brains more, things are going to get more interesting.

Three basic strands of research and investigation are relevant:

First, we are creating *artificial intelligence*. Currently, little in AI corresponds to the causal-physical functioning of the human brain. That functioning—from which our mental lives arise—currently gets instantiated by neurons, which are vastly different from, say, microprocessors. Still, progress in areas like machine learning is impressive and accelerating.

Second, we are making strides in *neuroscience*. We have not come terribly close to closing the explanatory gap between consciousness and the physics of the brain, body, and world, but we are learning more and more about the brain's architecture, neurochemistry, and function. We can operate on someone's brain or treat it with drugs. We have a long way to go, however, before we can synthesize a mind that experiences pain, pleasure, or wonder.

Third, we are getting better at *collective intelligence*. With the development of programmable incentives and peer technologies, we are becoming more connected and getting better at collaboration. Improved collective intelligence has downsides, but we are moving closer to the social singularity as we figure out how to coordinate the activities of our charged, gray jelly sacks.

Now, imagine these three relatively separate strands moving forward in time. As we move toward new time horizons, we can see that these strands are moving closer to one another. The punchline here is only a hypothesis: Eventually the strands will weave together. Philosophy will always stand there like Gandalf to warn of too much hubris or too many leaps of logic. Still, artificial intelligence, neuroscience, and collective intelligence will not remain distinct categories but eventually will converge.

From a big-picture perspective, the issue is how humans and AI can interface and, eventually, merge to some degree. Currently, significant differences exist between us, so the lingering question turns on what we might call "interoperability."

Some cognitive and brain scientists have warned AI researchers, rightly I think, that there are a whole lot of gaps to be bridged before we can start to think about a direct, physical interface that can connect a human brain with an AI. Yes, we are both causal-physical entities. But right now, that is mostly where the comparisons end.

Human beings are analog; AI is (so far) digital. The way our brains store memories is totally different from the precise memory addresses of computers. Neither the software nor the hardware of AI corresponds precisely to either the mind or the brain. And a brain is far more self-organizing as compared with current AI, although this could quickly change. There are many differences, and these differences make certain kinds of interface somewhat problematic.

Perhaps we should not assume any sufficiently advanced AI of the future will be neuromorphic. However, if it is, that could help not only with creating conscious machines but with how we interface with them.

Yes, humans interface with each other through language. And humans interface with computers through code. But if we were to attempt to connect human intelligence with machine cognition, finding translation standards between modes of operation could continue to elude us.

To bridge gaps between brains and machines, we will need to improve our understanding along a number of dimensions. But these problems are not insuperable. As long as everything there is to know about these threads of inquiry is knowable in principle, we can expect to make great leaps in coming decades.

Simply put, when robots are capable of taking all our jobs, the line between human and robot will have already blurred.

Will we be able to access databases with our thoughts? Will we be able to download others' memories, email thoughts, or experience the sensory inputs of others by proxy? Is consciousness and selfhood restricted to embodied brains, or will we learn to instantiate these properties in artificial jellies, pseudo-synaptic connections, or some other host stuff? Tearing down the categories of selfhood, consciousness, and the physical constraints of our humanity will open possibilities that could land us squarely between science fiction and some stranger notion of heaven.

It's not merely that we will connect ourselves through technology. It could also be possible to dissolve the "I," to visit the "not-I," and to open the doors of another's perception.

Within our lifetimes, perhaps, we will learn greater empathy through suspending our assumptions or even expanding current limits of mind, brain, and machine. We are, after all, attempting to rewrite the human source code. And in the social singularity we will coalesce, reconstituting ourselves like some advanced coral reef teeming in an ocean of space dust. We will expand outward into the cosmos until we discover the whole universe was within each of us all along, and we were never alone.

ACKNOWLEDGMENTS

I would like first to thank Justin and Jessica Arman for their financial support for this publication. Without them, the book might have existed only on a server somewhere, lost in time. I owe Justin additional thanks for his belief in me as a thinker, writer, and iconoclast, and also for his faith in me as one capable of building something lasting.

Thanks also go to my wife, Carly, for patience with me during those countless hours with my head in a laptop or in the clouds. Without Carly's support, this project would not have been possible.

This work was also made possible by financial support of the Robert and Marie Hansen Foundation, whose seed donation brought Social Evolution, the organization under whose auspices this book was written, into existence. (Social Evolution is a 501(c)(3) nonprofit organization under the US tax code.)

Thanks go also to Social Evolution's board of directors, including James Anderson, Matt McKibbin, Colin Pape, Michael Strong, and especially Joel Dusoe, whose moral support has been invaluable. Former trustee John Guido deserves appreciation for help during our liftoff phase.

Appreciation also goes to the Foundation for Economic Education, for which I originally wrote many passages that were repurposed in this book. I have been both a writer and an editor for this august organization. FEE allows republication under a Creative Commons license that more or less means republication is allowed with credit to FEE. This serves not only as that due credit but as sincere thanks for years of letting me put boundary-pushing content out under FEE's banner.

Finally, I owe debts of thanks to Casper Craven, Shannon Ewing, Justin Goro, John Papola, Barry Rand, Sid Borders, Felix Borders, Moritz Bierling, James Wallman, Gian Piero de Bellis, Robert Himber, Alexander R. Cohen, Weston Woodward, Alex Torres, Katherine MacLellan, Joe Quirk, Jason Rink, and many others who've given generously of their time, resources, and encouragement.

Alexander R. Cohen and Robert Himber receive special acknowledgment for helping the manuscript shine as editors.

The cover was designed by Trivuj and Starline. Alexander R. Cohen laid out the interior.

NOTES

1   Jorge Luis Borges, "Garden of the Forking Paths," in *Collected Fictions*, trans. Andrew Hurley (London: Penguin, 1999), 67.

2   Alvin and Heidi Toffler warned in their book *Future Shock* that the rate of change might increase to a point beyond human beings' ability to cope with said change. Alvin Toffler and Heidi Toffler, *Future Shock* (New York: Random House, 1984).

3   Wallace Stevens, "The Idea of Order at Key West," in The *Collected Poems of Wallace Stevens* (New York: Vintage Books, 1990), 128.

4   Guy Debord, *Society of the Spectacle* (Detroit: Black & Red, 1970), 60.

5   444 Parl. Deb., H.C. (5th ser.) (1947) col. 206–07 (Winston Churchill, M.P.).

6   Robert Kurzban, John Tooby, and Leda Cosmides, "Can Race Be Erased? Coalitional Computation and Social Categorization," *Proceedings of the National Academy of Sciences of the United States of America* 98, no. 26 (December 18, 2001), https://doi.org/10.1073/pnas.251541498.

7   Trevor Burrus, "'Tis the Season for Politics to Make Us Worse," Cato Institute, December 25, 2014, https://www.cato.org/publications /commentary/tis-season-politics-make-us-worse.

8   Burrus, "'Tis the Season."

9   Jason Brennan, *Against Democracy* (Princeton, NJ: Princeton University Press, 2017), 4.

10   Brennan, *Against Democracy*, 5.

11   Brennan, *Against Democracy*, 5.

12   Clay Shirky, "There's No Such Thing as a Protest Vote," Medium, August 6, 2016, https://medium.com/@cshirky/theres-no-such-thing-as -a-protest-vote-c2fdacabd704.

13   John W. Schoen, "Economic Issues Could Turn These Swing-State Votes in the 2016 Election," NBC News, August 7, 2016, https://www.nbcnews.com/business/economy/economic-issues-could -turn-these-swing-state-votes-2016-election-n623661.

14   Jim Pagels, "You're Just as Likely to Die en Route to Vote than to Impact an Election Outcome," *Forbes*, November 14, 2014, https://www.forbes.com/sites/jimpagels/2014/11/04/youre-just-as-likely -to-die-en-route-to-vote-than-to-impact-an-election-outcome/.

15   Jason Brennan, "If You Don't Vote, You Have No Right to Complain," *Bleeding Heart Libertarians*, October 30, 2014, http://bleedingheartlibertarians.com/2014/10/if-you-dont-vote-you-have -no-right-to-complain/.

16   Michael Munger, "Unicorn Governance," FEE.org, August 11, 2014, https://fee.org/articles/unicorn-governance/.

17   Michael Munger, "Unicorn Governance."

18   K Street in Washington, DC, is where many lobbyists have offices.

19   Ronald Bailey, "Broken Science," *Reason*, February 2016, http://reason.com/archives/2016/01/19/broken-science.

20 James M. Buchanan, "Public Choice: Politics Without Romance," *Policy* 19, no. 3 (Spring 2003): 15, https://www.cis.org.au/app/uploads/2015/04 /images/stories/policy-magazine/2003-spring/2003-19-3-james-m -buchanan.pdf.

21 Buchanan, "Public Choice," 15.

22 James Madison, "Federalist No. 10," in George W. Carey and James McClellan, eds., *The Federalist Papers* (Indianapolis, IN: Liberty Fund, 2001), 42–49.

23 Deirdre McCloskey refers to the "Great Fact" in a number of essays and in her book *Bourgeois Dignity: Why Economics Can't Explain the Modern World* (Chicago: University of Chicago Press, 2014), 558.

24 Ferris Jabr, "Steven Pinker: Humans Are Less Violent than Ever," *New Scientist*, October 12, 2011, https://www.newscientist.com/article/mg21228340-100-steven-pinker -humans-are-less-violent-than-ever/.

25 Jabr, "Steven Pinker."

26 Yaneer Bar-Yam, "Complexity Rising: From Human Beings to Human Civilization, a Complexity Profile," New England Complex Systems Institute, December 1997, http://www.necsi.edu/projects/yaneer/Civilization.html.

27 Yaneer Bar-Yam, "Complexity Rising."

28 Yaneer Bar-Yam, "Complexity Rising."

29 James C. Scott, *Two Cheers for Anarchism: Six Easy Pieces on Autonomy, Dignity, and Meaningful Work and Play* (Princeton, NJ: Princeton University Press, 2014), 14.

30 James C. Scott, *Two Cheers for Anarchism*, 22.

31 Carl Bernstein, "The CIA and the Media: How America's Most Powerful News Media Worked Hand in Glove with the Central Intelligence Agency and Why the Church Committee Covered It Up," Carl Bernstein, accessed April 11, 2018, http://www.carlbernstein.com/magazine_cia_and_media.php.

32 Operation Mockingbird was a large-scale program of the US Central Intelligence Agency (CIA) that began in the early 1950s and sought to manipulate news media.

33 Walter Cronkite was a beloved newsreader who appeared on the nightly news for decades.

34 Edward Bernays, *Propaganda* (New York: Ig Publishing, 2004), 4.

35 Jordan Greenhall, "Understanding the Blue Church," *Deep Code*, Medium, March 30, 2017, https://medium.com/deep-code/understanding -the-blue-church-e4781b2bd9b5.

36 Greenhall, "Understanding the Blue Church."

37 Greenhall, "Understanding the Blue Church."

38 Jeff Giesea, "It's Time to Embrace Memetic Warfare," *OPEN Publications* 1, no. 5 (Spring 2017): 7, https://docs.wixstatic.com/ugd /b3eb9d_e9b753fb75fe45fa8e05afea81bca8ce.pdf. The copyright page of the PDF file notes that it is a reprint of a 2015 document.

39 Disclosure: Chris Rufer is a friend, and I have been lucky enough to undertake a venture with him as an investor.

40 Max Borders, "Enterprise without Bosses: An Interview with Paul Green, Jr.," FEE.org, February 21, 2013, https://fee.org/articles /enterprise-without-bosses-an-interview-with-paul-green-jr/.

41 Borders, "Enterprise without Bosses."

42   Yanis Varoufakis, "Why Valve? Or, What Do We Need Corporations for
      and How Does Valve's Management Structure Fit into Today's Corporate
      World?" *Valve Economics*, August 3, 2012, http://blogs.valvesoftware
      .com/economics/why-valve-or-what-do-we-need-corporations-for-and-
      how-does-valves-management-structure-fit-into-todays-corporate-
      world/.

43   Brian J. Robertson, *Holacracy: The New Management System for a
      Rapidly Changing World* (New York: Henry Holt, 2015), 26.

44   Lynne Kiesling, "Hayek on Order: Cosmos and Taxis," *Knowledge
      Problem*, December 4, 2003,
      https://knowledgeproblem.com/2003/12/04/hayek_on_order/.

45   Kiesling, "Hayek on Order."

46   Philip Tetlock, "Why Foxes Are Better Forecasters than Hedgehogs,"
      Long Now Foundation, January 26, 2007, http://longnow.org/seminars
      /02007/jan/26/why-foxes-are-better-forecasters-than-hedgehogs/.

47   Jessica Firger, "Science's Reproducibility Problem: 100 Psych Studies
      Were Tested and Only Half Held Up," *Newsweek*, August 28, 2015,
      http://www.newsweek.com/reproducibility-science-psychology-studies
      -366744.

48   Jenna Robinson, "How Government Makes Us Fatter," FEE.org,
      December 28, 2012, https://fee.org/articles/how-government-makes-us
      -fatter/.

49   Anahad O'Connor, "Study Questions Fat and Heart Disease Link," *Well*
      (blog), *New York Times*, March 17, 2014, https://well.blogs.nytimes.com
      /2014/03/17/study-questions-fat-and-heart-disease-link/.

50   Ronald Bailey, "Broken Science," *Reason*, February 2016,
      http://reason.com/archives/2016/01/19/broken-science.

51   Richard Horton, "Offline: What Is Medicine's 5 Sigma?" *Lancet* 385, no.
       9976 (April 11, 2015): 1380,
       https://doi.org/10.1016/s0140-6736(15)60696-1.

52   C. G. Begley and Lee M. Ellis, "Raise Standards for Preclinical Cancer
       Research," *Nature* 483, no. 7391 (March 2012): 531–533,
       https://doi.org/10.1038/483531a.

53   Yudhijit Bhattacharjee, "The Mind of a Con Man," *New York Times
       Magazine*, April 26, 2013,
       http://www.nytimes.com/2013/04/28/magazine/diederik-stapels
       -audacious-academic-fraud.html?pagewanted=all&_r=1.

54   Asit K. Biswas and Julian Kirchherr, "Prof, No One Is Reading You,"
       Straits Times, April 11, 2015, http://www.straitstimes.com/opinion/prof
       -no-one-is-reading-you.

55   Rose Eveleth, "Academics Write Papers Arguing over How Many People
       Read (and Cite) Their Papers," *Smithsonian*, March 25, 2014,
       https://www.smithsonianmag.com/smart-news/half-academic-studies-are
       -never-read-more-three-people-180950222/.

56   This quote by Richard Cornuelle comes by way of Lenore Ealy,
       president of the Philanthropic Enterprise, an organization built to further
       the legacy and thinking of Richard Cornuelle. While the original source
       of the quote is unpublished, Ealy shares the quote with permission of the
       Philanthropic Enterprise, which archives Cornuelle's work.

57   Michael Polanyi, "The Republic of Science," Center for Science &
       Technology Policy Research, accessed at a URL where it no longer is.
       This article was published at *Minerva* 1, no. 1 (September 1962): 54–74.

58   Jordan Greenhall, "Understanding the Blue Church," *Deep Code*,
       Medium, March 30, 2017, https://medium.com/deep-code/understanding
       -the-blue-church-e4781b2bd9b5.

59   John Taylor Gatto, *Dumbing Us Down: The Hidden Curriculum of Compulsory Schooling* (Gabriola Island, BC: New Society Publishers, 2005), 10.

60   Olga Syutkin and Pavel Syutkin, "Fried Eggs with Jam? A history of the Soviet Union through Its Food," *Guardian*, October 15, 2015, https://www.theguardian.com/world/2015/oct/15/cccp-cookbook-short -history-of-the-ussr-through-its-food.

61   Jordan Greenhall, "Understanding the Blue Church."

62   Michael Strong, "About Michael Strong," *The Purpose of Education*, accessed April 11, 2018, https://thepurposeofeducation.wordpress.com/about-michael-strong/.

63   Learning Is Earning, accessed April 11, 2018, http://www.learningisearning2026.org/.

64   Max Shapiro, *The Penniless Billionaires* (New York: Times Books, 1980), 23.

65   Lawrence W. Reed and Marc Hyden, "Rome: Money, Mischief and Minted Crises," FEE.org, May 21, 2015, https://fee.org/articles/rome -money-mischief-and-minted-crises.

66   Satoshi Nakamoto, "Bitcoin: A Peer-to-Peer Electronic Cash System," Bitcoin.org, January 9, 2009, https://bitcoin.org/bitcoin.pdf.

67   F. A. Hayek, *Denationalisation of Money: The Argument Refined; An Analysis of the Theory and Practice of Concurrent Currencies*, 3rd ed. (London: Institute of Economic Affairs, 1990), 23, http://nakamotoinstitute.org/static/docs/denationalisation.pdf.

68   "What Are the Goals of U.S. Monetary Policy?" U.S. Monetary Policy: An Introduction, Federal Reserve Bank of San Francisco, last updated February 6, 2004, https://www.frbsf.org/education/teacher-resources/us -monetary-policy-introduction/goals/.

69 Daniel Krawisz, "Hyperbitcoinization," Satoshi Nakamoto Institute, March 29, 2014, http://nakamotoinstitute.org/mempool/hyperbitcoinization/.

70 Daniel Krawisz, "Hyperbitcoinization."

71 Daniel Krawisz, "Hyperbitcoinization."

72 Justin Goro, "The Great Hard Fork: An Unraveling of State Legitimacy," *Social Evolution*, Medium, December 7, 2017, https://medium.com /social-evolution/the-great-hard-fork-an-unraveling-of-state-legitimacy-a559b7d125ed.

73 Justin Goro, "The Great Hard Fork."

74 Justin Goro, "The Great Hard Fork."

75 Justin Goro, "The Great Hard Fork."

76 Justin Goro, "The Great Hard Fork."

77 For a glimpse of how we might develop mutual aid systems in the cloud, see Max Borders, "How We Become the Social Safety Net," *Social Evolution*, Medium, February 26, 2018, https://medium.com/social -evolution/how-we-become-the-social-safety-net-2994a68a53db.

78 Eric Hughes, "A Cypherpunk's Manifesto," Activism.net, March 9, 1993, accessed at a URL where it no longer is.

79 "Disruptive Innovations," Christensen Institute, accessed April 11, 2018, https://www.christenseninstitute.org/disruptive-innovations/.

80 Ulam Stanislaw, "Tribute to John von Neumann," *Bulletin of the American Mathematical Society* 64, no. 3 (May 1958), doi:10.1007/springerreference_72784, https://docs.google.com/file/d/0B -5-JeCa2Z7hbWcxTGsyU09HSTg/edit?pli=1.

81   Quoted in Vernor Vinge, "The Coming Technological Singularity," 1993,
      https://edoras.sdsu.edu/~vinge/misc/singularity.html.

82   Vinge, "The Coming Technological Singularity."

83   Bill Joy, "Why the Future Doesn't Need Us," *Wired*, April 1, 2000,
      https://www.wired.com/2000/04/joy-2/.

84   Bill Joy, "Why the Future Doesn't Need Us."

85   I'll leave it to others and let the titans criticize by creating. That is, they
      can create ventures like Musk's Neuralink, which is intended to head the
      most dystopian futures off at the pass by creating a robust brain-
      computer interface.

86   At this writing, Google estimates 10,800 results for the query, "'We
      shape our tools and then our tools shape us' McLuhan." However, the
      first result is from the website *Quote Investigator*, which had "not yet
      found any evidence that McLuhan claimed coinage of the adage."
      According to *QI*, John M. Culkin, in an article about McLuhan's views,
      wrote, "We shape our tools and thereafter they shape us." *QI* suggests
      that the saying evolved from a line by Winston Churchill in a speech on
      rebuilding the chamber of the House of Commons after the Blitz of
      London: "We shape our buildings and afterwards our buildings shape
      us." Garson O'Toole, "We Shape Our Tools, and Thereafter Our Tools
      Shape Us, *Quote Investigator*, June 26, 2016,
      https://quoteinvestigator.com/2016/06/26/shape/, quoting John M.
      Culkin, "A Schoolman's Guide to Marshall McLuhan," *Saturday Review*,
      March 18, 1967, 70, via Unz, and 393 Parl. Deb., H.C. (5th ser.) (1943)
      col. 403–73 (Winston Churchill, M.P.), https://api.parliament.uk/historic
      -hansard/commons/1943/oct/28/house-of-commons-rebuilding.

87   John B. Geijsbeek, *Ancient Double-Entry Bookkeeping: Lucas Pacioli's
      Treatise* (Charleston, SC: Nabu Press, 2010), 33.

88   Douglass C. North, "Economic Performance Through Time" (Lecture to
      the Memory of Alfred Nobel, December 9, 1993), http://www.nobelprize
      .org/nobel_prizes/economic-sciences/laureates/1993/north-lecture.html.

89 "Lying Commies," *Economist*, July 19, 2014, https://www.economist
.com/news/finance-and-economics/21607830-more-people-are-exposed
-socialism-worse-they-behave-lying-commies.

90 "Lying Commies."

91 Bradley Campbell and Jason Manning, "Microagressions and Moral
Cultures," ResearchGate, uploaded April 19, 2018, https://www
.researchgate.net/profile/Jason_Manning2/publication/272408166
_Microaggression_and_Moral_Cultures/links/5ad8d083458515c60f5a5e
c5/Microaggression-and-Moral-Cultures.pdf. The article was published
at *Comparative Sociology* 13, no. 6 (2014): 692–726.

92 Campbell and Manning, "Microagressions and Moral Cultures," 29.

93 Campbell and Manning, "Microagressions and Moral Cultures," 29–30.

94 Campbell and Manning, "Microagressions and Moral Cultures," 31.

95 Max Borders, "The Origins of Envy," American Enterprise Institute,
January 14, 2012, http://www.aei.org/publication/the-origins-of-envy/.

96 Deirdre N. McCloskey, "What's Still Wrong with Marxism: Some
Fragments on a Theme," Deirdre N. McCloskey, January 25, 2014,
http://www.deirdremccloskey.com/docs/pdf/NebraskaSeminar.pdf.

97 Adam Thierer, "Embracing a Culture of Permissionless Innovation,"
Cato Institute, November 17, 2014, https://www.cato.org/publications
/cato-online-forum/embracing-culture-permissionless-innovation.

98 Daniel C. Dennett, *Intuition Pumps and Other Tools for Thinking* (2013;
repr. New York: W. W. Norton, 2014), 203,
https://books.google.com/books?isbn=0393348784.

99 Nick Szabo, "Jurisdiction as Property: The Paper," *Unenumerated*, June
3, 2006, http://unenumerated.blogspot.co.uk/2006/06/jurisdiction-as
-property-paper.html.

100   Lenore T. Ealy, "Exit, Voice, and Bourbon," FEE.org, April 3, 2013,
       https://fee.org/articles/exit-voice-and-bourbon/.

101   Full disclosure: As an early scholar with the Seasteading Institute, I got
       to participate in creating the intellectual foundations of this movement.
       I'd like to think of myself as a minor "founding father" of seasteading.

102   Seasteading Institute, "Government of French Polynesia Signs
       Agreement with Seasteaders for Floating Island Project," January 17,
       2017, https://www.seasteading.org/government-french-polynesia-signs
       -agreement-seasteaders-floating-island-project/.

103   Matt Ridley, *The Rational Optimist: How Prosperity Evolves*, (New
       York: Harper Perennial, 2010), 1.

104   Matt Ridley, *The Evolution of Everything* (New York: Harper Collins,
       2015), 123.

105   Matt Ridley, *The Evolution of Everything*, 123.

106   Steven Johnson, "The Genius of the Tinkerer," *Wall Street Journal*,
       September 24, 2010, https://www.wsj.com/articles
       /SB10001424052748703989304575503730101860838.

107   Steven Johnson, "The Genius of the Tinkerer."

108   B. Joseph Pine II and James H. Gilmore, "Welcome to the Experience
       Economy," *Harvard Business Review*, July–August 1998,
       https://hbr.org/1998/07/welcome-to-the-experience-economy.

109   James Surowiecki, "Robots Won't Take All Our Jobs," *Wired*, August 16,
       2017, https://www.wired.com/2017/08/robots-will-not-take-your-job/.

110   Henry Hazlitt, *Economics in One Lesson,* special edition for the
       Foundation for Economic Education (New York: Pocket Books, 1952),
       32.

111   Susie Cranston and Scott Keller, "Increasing the 'Meaning Quotient' of Work," *McKinsey Quarterly*, January 2013, https://www.mckinsey.com/business-functions/organization/our-insights/increasing-the-meaning-quotient-of-work.

112   Thomas Nagel, "What is it like to be a bat?" in *The Nature of Mind*, ed. David M. Rosenthal (New York: Oxford University Press, 1991), 422–28. This classic essay was originally published at *Philosophical Review* 83, no. 4 (October 1974): 435–50, and it appears in Nagel's book *Mortal Questions* (Cambridge: Cambridge University Press, 2012).

113   Chelsea Gohd, "New Research Links Human Consciousness to a Law That Governs the Universe," *Futurism*, January 31, 2018, https://futurism.com/new-study-links-human-consciousness-law-governs-universe/.

114   Jonathan Haidt, *The Righteous Mind: Why Good People Are Divided by Politics and Religion* (New York: Vintage Books), 53.

115   Lisa Cron, *Wired for Story: The Writer's Guide to Using Brain Science to Hook Readers from the Very First Sentence* (Berkeley, CA: Ten Speed Press, 2012), 45.

116   Daniel Gilbert, *Stumbling on Happiness* (New York: Knopf Doubleday, 2006), 71.

117   B. Joseph Pine and James H. Gilmore, "Welcome to the Experience Economy," *Harvard Business Review*, July–August 1998, https://hbr.org/1998/07/welcome-to-the-experience-economy.

118   Dominique Afacan, "Stuffocation—an Interview with James Wallman," *Forbes*, January 23, 2014, https://www.forbes.com/sites/dominiqueafacan/2014/01/23/stuffocation-an-interview-with-james-wallman/.

119   Robyn G. Lawrence, "Wabi-Sabi: The Art of Imperfection," *Utne Reader*, September 2001, https://www.utne.com/mind-and-body/wabi-sabi.

120   Chris Anderson, "About Me," *Long Tail*, archived February 4, 2018,
       available via https://tinyurl.com/y4q687o6.

121   "Van Gogh Painting Sold for $111 Million at Auction," *Straits Times*,
       November 14, 2017, http://www.straitstimes.com/lifestyle/arts/van-gogh
       -painting-sold-for-111-million-at-auction.

122   This heuristic is synthesized from Joseph Pine II "Multiverse" (lecture,
       Mobile Monday Amsterdam, video published January 31, 2010),
       https://www.youtube.com/watch?v=FKrNKblbxDQ.

123   Steve Bramucci, "Why You Need a Microadventure—Today More than
       Ever," *Uproxx*, November 28, 2017, https://uproxx.com/life/outside
       -nature-political-fatigue/.

124   Aristotle, *Politics*, trans. Benjamin Jowett, in *The Complete Works of
       Aristotle: The Revised Oxford Translation*, ed. Jonathan Barnes
       (Princeton, NJ: Princeton University Press, 1984), 2:1988.

125   David Beito, "From Mutual Aid to Welfare State: How Fraternal
       Societies Fought Poverty and Taught Character," Heritage.org, July 27,
       2000, https://www.heritage.org/political-process/report/mutual-aid
       -welfare-state-how-fraternal-societies-fought-poverty-and-taught.

126   Tracy McVeigh, "For Japan's 'stranded singles,' virtual love beats the
       real thing," *Guardian*, November 19, 2016,
       https://www.theguardian.com/world/2016/nov/20/japan-stranded
       -singles-virtual-love.

127   Bijoy Goswami, "The Meaning Matrix: How to 'Know Thyself' in a
       Chaotic World" (lecture, Voice & Exit Conference & Festival, November
       11, 2016), https://www.voiceandexit.com/2016-videos/meaning-matrix
       -know-thyself-chaotic-world/.

128   James Vincent, "Elon Musk Says We Need to Regulate AI before It
       Becomes a Danger to Humanity," *Verge*, July 27, 2017,
       https://www.theverge.com/2017/7/17/15980954/elon-musk-ai-regulation
       -existential-threat.

129 Timothy B. Lee, "William Baumol, Whose Famous Economic Theory Explains the Modern World, Has Died," *Vox*, May 4, 2017, https://www.vox.com/new-money/2017/5/4/15547364/baumol-cost -disease-explained.

130 Italo Calvino, *Invisible Cities* (Orlando, FL: Harcourt, Brace, 1974), 88.

131 Quoted in Steven Johnson, *Emergence: The Connected Lives of Ants, Brains, Cities, and Software* (New York: Scribner, 2012), 27.

132 Jane Jacobs, *The Death and Life of American Cities* (New York: Random House, 1961), 15.

133 Maria Bustillos, "You Don't Understand Bitcoin because You Think Money Is Real," Medium, November 30, 2017, https://medium.com/@mariabustillos/you-dont-understand-bitcoin -because-you-think-money-is-real-5aef45b8e952.

134 Nick Szabo, "Bit Gold," *Unenumerated*, December 27, 2008, http://unenumerated.blogspot.com/2005/12/bit-gold.html.

135 Nick Szabo, "Jurisdiction as Property: The Paper," *Unenumerated*, June 3, 2006, http://unenumerated.blogspot.co.uk/2006/06/jurisdiction-as -property-paper.html.

136 Szabo, "Jurisdiction as Property."

137 Szabo, "Jurisdiction as Property."

138 Andreas M. Antonopoulos, "Decentralization: Why Dumb Networks Are Better," FEE.org, March 4, 2015, https://fee.org/articles/decentralization -why-dumb-networks-are-better/.

139 Mike Gibson, "The Nakamoto Consensus—How We End Bad Governance," *Let a Thousand Nations Bloom*, April 3, 2015, https://athousandnations.com/2015/04/03/the-nakamoto-consensus %E2%80%8A-%E2%80%8Ahow-we-end-bad-governance/.

140 Chris Berg, Sinclair Davidson, and Jason Potts, "The Blockchain Economy: A Beginner's Guide to Institutional Cryptoeconomics," Medium, September 26, 2017, https://medium.com/@cryptoeconomics /the-blockchain-economy-a-beginners-guide-to-institutional -cryptoeconomics-64bf2f2beec4.

141 Ameer Rosic, "Smart Contracts: The Blockchain Technology that Will Replace Lawyers," Blockgeeks, 2016. https://blockgeeks.com/guides/smart-contracts/.

142 Rob Knight, "Why the Biggest Winners of the Blockchain Might Be Economists," *Humanizing the Singularity*, Medium, January 2, 2018, https://medium.com/humanizing-the-singularity/why-the-biggest -winners-of-the-blockchain-might-be-economists-60b9c67f47b4.

143 Justin Goro, "Bitcoin Has Turned the Human Race into a Hive Mind Super Computer," *Social Evolution*, Medium, October 24, 2017, https://medium.com/social-evolution/bitcoin-has-turned-the-human-race- into-a-hive-mind-super-computer-6668739fdddb.

144 Justin Goro, "Bitcoin Has Turned the Human Race into a Hive Mind Super Computer."

145 I heard Brock Pierce give a version of this explanation at Burning Man, Camp Decentral, August 2017. This is my interpretation of what I heard.

146 Alex Tabarrok, "Making Markets Work Better: Dominant Assurance Contracts and Some Other Helpful Ideas," *Cato Unbound*, June 7, 2017, https://www.cato-unbound.org/2017/06/07/alex-tabarrok/making -markets-work-better-dominant-assurance-contracts-some-other-helpful.

147 Arthur Brock, "Cryptocurrencies Are Dead," *MetaCurrency Project*, Medium, September 15, 2016, https://medium.com/metacurrency-project /cryptocurrencies-are-dead-d4223154d783.

148 Matt Ridley, "Why Selecting Intelligent Babies Won't Happen," *Matt Ridley Online Blog*, December 29, 2017, http://rationaloptimist.com/blog/designer-babies-and-iq/.

149   Yaneer Bar-Yam, "Teams: A Manifesto," *Complex Systems Channel*,
       Medium, July 31, 2016, https://medium.com/complex-systems-channel
       /teams-a-manifesto-7490eab144fa.

150   Vincent Ostrom, *The Political Theory of a Compound Republic:
       Designing the American Experiment*, 3rd ed., including material
       coauthored with Barbara Allen (New York: Rowman & Littlefield 1971),
       138.

151   Daniel I. Mitchell, "Five reasons Why Switzerland Is Better than the
       United States (but Five Reasons Why I'll Stay in America)," Daniel I.
       Mitchell, March 14, 2011, https://danieljmitchell.wordpress.com/2011/03
       /14/five-reasons-why-switzerland-is-better-than-the-united-states-but
       -five-reasons-why-ill-stay-in-america/.

152   "It would be unfortunate if a politically correct progressivism were to
       deny the reality of the challenge to social solidarity posed by diversity,"
       Robert Putnam concluded in 2007, shocking the author as much as it did
       the social science world. "It would be equally unfortunate if an
       ahistorical and ethnocentric conservatism were to deny that addressing
       that challenge is both feasible and desirable." Robert D. Putnam, "E
       Pluribus Unum: Diversity and Community in the Twenty-First Century,"
       Scandinavian Political Studies 30, no. 2 (June 2007): 137,
       https://doi.org/10.1111/j.1467-9477.2007.00176.x.

153   Thomas Jefferson to Gideon Granger, August 13, 1800, Founders Online,
       National Archives, last modified April 12, 2018, https://founders
       .archives.gov/documents/Jefferson/01-32-02-0061. Punctuation,
       capitalization, and the like have been modernized.

154   Thomas Jefferson, Inaugural Address, in Adrienne Koch and William
       Peden, eds., *The Life and Selected Writings of Thomas Jefferson* (New
       York: Random House, 1993), 300.

155   Sarah Rabi, review of *The State in the Third Millenium*, by Hans-Adam
       II, *Vienna Review*, May 1, 2010, archived April 6, 2015, available via
       https://tinyurl.com/y63bxcpo.

156 Tom W. Bell, *Your Next Government? From the Nation State to Stateless Nations* (Cambridge: Cambridge University Press, 2018), 23.

157 Jamie Bartlett, "Return of the City-State," *Aeon*, September 5, 2017, https://aeon.co/essays/the-end-of-a-world-of-nation-states-may-be-upon-us.

158 James Madison, "Federalist No. 51," in George W. Carey and James McClellan, eds., *The Federalist Papers* (Indianapolis, IN: Liberty Fund, 2001), 264–272.

159 Joe Quirk, *Seasteading: How Floating Nations Will Restore the Environment, Enrich the Poor, Cure the Sick, and Liberate Humanity from Politicians* (New York: Free Press, 2017), 30.

160 Patri Friedman and Brad Taylor, "Seasteading: Striking at the Root of Bad Government," FEE.org, February 24, 2011, https://fee.org/articles/seasteading-striking-at-the-root-of-bad-government/.

161 Nassim Nicholas Taleb, *Antifragile: Things that Gain from Disorder* (New York: Random House Trade Paperbacks, 2012), 349.

162 Diego Espinosa, "Time to Design Our Networks (Because Science)," Medium, May 12, 2016, https://medium.com/@dvespinosa/time-to-design-our-networks-6a412459f46c.

163 Zach Weinersmith, *Polystate: A Thought Experiment in Distributed Government* (self-pub., Amazon Digital Services, 2013), Kindle.

164 Zach Weinersmith, *Polystate*.

165 Variations on this section were originally published on *Let a Thousand Nations Bloom* and Panarchy.org.

166 Paul-Emile de Puydt, "Panarchy," trans. John Zube et al., Panarchy.org, revised May 2006, https://www.panarchy.org/depuydt/1860.eng.html.

167 Charles Joseph Marie Ghislain de Brouckère, review of Paul-Emile de Puydt, "Panarchy," *The Belgian Economist: Organ of the Interests of Industry and Trade*, August 4, 1860, 503.

168 De Brouckère, review of "Panarchy," 503.

169 Quoted in Arnold Kling, "I Heart Steven Pinker," *Permanent Link* (blog), Library of Economics and Liberty, October 12, 2006, http://econlog.econlib.org/archives/2006/10/i_heart_steven.html.

170 Tyler Cowen, "Public Goods," in David R. Henderson, ed., *The Concise Encyclopedia of Economics* (n.p.: Liberty Fund, 2008), http://www.econlib.org/library/Enc/PublicGoods.html.

171 Deirdre N. McCloskey, "Language and Interest in the Economy: A White Paper on 'Humanomics,'" SSRN, August 12, 2011, https://doi.org/10.2139/ssrn.1889320.

172 Kevin McPherson and Bruce Wright, "Gone to Texas: Migration," Texas Comptroller of Public Accounts, October 2017, https://comptroller.texas.gov/economy/fiscal-notes/2017/october/migration.php

173 Tom W. Bell, *Your Next Government? From the Nation State to Stateless Nations* (Cambridge: Cambridge University Press, 2018), 127.

174 Robert Nozick, *Anarchy, State, and Utopia* (New York: Penguin Books, 2013), 316.

175 Frederick Jackson Turner, *The Frontier in American History*, (Mineola, New York: Dover Publications, 1996), 38.

176 Michael P. Gibson, "The Nakamoto Consensus—How We End Bad Governance," *Let a Thousand Nations Bloom*, April 3, 2015, https://athousandnations.com/2015/04/03/the-nakamoto-consensus%E2%80%8A-%E2%80%8Ahow-we-end-bad-governance/.

177 Gibson, "The Nakamoto Consensus."

178 Richard Rorty, *Contingency, Irony, and Solidarity* (Cambridge: Cambridge University Press, 1989), 192.

179 R. R. Griffiths et al., "Mystical-Type Experiences Occasioned by Psilocybin Mediate the Attribution of Personal Meaning and Spiritual Significance 14 Months Later," *Journal of Psychopharmacology* 22, no. 6 (2008): 1, https://doi.org/10.1177/0269881108094300. Emphases added.

180 Taylor Lyons and Robin L. Carhart-Harris, "Increased Nature Relatedness and Decreased Authoritarian Political Views after Psilocybin for Treatment-Resistant Depression," *Journal of Psychopharmacology*, published ahead of print, January 17, 2018, https://doi.org/10.1177/0269881117748902.

181 Leonard E. Read, *Elements of Libertarian Leadership: Notes on the Theory, Methods, and Practice of Freedom* (Irvington-on-Hudson, NY: Foundation for Economic Education, 1962), 43–44, https://fee-misc.s3.amazonaws.com/files/docLib/ElementsofLibertarianLeadership.pdf.

182 Justin Goro, "Bitcoin Has Turned the Human Race into a Hive Mind Super Computer," *Social Evolution*, Medium, October 24, 2017, https://medium.com/social-evolution/bitcoin-has-turned-the-human-race-into-a-hive-mind-super-computer-6668739fdddb.

183 Goro, "Bitcoin Has Turned the Human Race into a Hive Mind Super Computer."

184 Steven Kotler and Jamie Wheal, *Stealing Fire: How Silicon Valley, the Navy SEALS, and Maverick Scientists Are Revolutionizing the Way We Live and Work* (New York: Dey Street Books, 2017), 68.

185 Kotler and Wheal, *Stealing Fire*, 68.

186 Christopher C. Cowan and Don E. Beck, *Spiral Dynamics* (Maiden, MA: Blackwell Publishing, 1996), 286.

187   This maxim, "Any sufficiently advanced technology is indistinguishable from magic," is attributed to science fiction author Arthur C. Clarke.

188   Clare W. Graves, "On the Theory of Ethical Behavior," on Chris Cowan, Natasha Todorovic, and William R. Lee's website Dr. Clare W. Graves, 2001, http://www.clarewgraves.com/articles_content/1961/1961d.htm.

189   Jonathan Haidt, *The Righteous Mind: Why Good People Are Divided by Politics and Religion* (New York: Vintage Books, 2013), xx–xi.

190   Ken Wilber, *A Theory of Everything: An Integral Vision for Business, Politics, Science and Spirituality* (Boston: Shambhala, 2001), 11.

191   Wilber, *A Theory of Everything*, 11.

192   Ken Wilber, "Trump and a Post-Truth World," *Integral Life*, January 2, 2017, https://integrallife.com/trump-post-truth-world/.

193   Natalie Angier, "Edward O. Wilson's New Take on Human Nature." *Smithsonian*, March 31, 2012, https://www.smithsonianmag.com/science-nature/edward-o-wilsons-new-take-on-human-nature-160810520/.

194   Christopher C. Cowan and Don E. Beck, *Spiral Dynamics* (Maiden, MA: Blackwell Publishing, 2006), 110, https://books.google.com/books?id=w7PwBwAAQBAJ. Superscripts replaced with hyphens.

195   I write this admitting that I am no guru. Indeed, I need to practice what I preach. I am pretty sure that the coming era will thrust many of us into our inner worlds, as we will need and thus seek out these sanctums.

196   E. O. Wilson, *On Human Nature* (Cambridge, MA: Harvard University Press, 2004), 6.

197   Jonathan Haidt, *The Righteous Mind: Why Good People Are Divided by Politics and Religion* (New York: Vintage Books, 2013), 366.

198 *The Bhagavad Gita* (Tomales, CA: The Blue Mountain Center of Meditation, 1985), 106.

Review Us

Please review us on Amazon! Your positive review will help us to rise in the rankings, which will help more people discover the book.

Support Social Evolution

Social Evolution is the organization that published the book. From inspiration to incubation, we want to do more good work.

You can join our email list by getting in touch at hello@social-evolution.com.

You also can support our foundation through various means—including cryptocurrencies—at social-evolution.com.

71038051R00115

Made in the USA
Columbia, SC
24 August 2019